MELISSA ETHERIDGE

*M*ELISSA *E*THERIDGE

CHRIS NICKSON

ST. MARTIN'S GRIFFIN
NEW YORK

All photos © D.M.I. Photography

Design by Nancy Resnick

Library of Congress Cataloging-in-Publication Data

Nickson, Chris.
 Melissa Etheridge / Chris Nickson.—1st St. Martin's Griffin ed.
  p.   cm.
 Discography: p. 145
 ISBN 0-312-15171-3
 1. Etheridge, Melissa. 2. Rock musicians—United States—Biography.
 3. Singers—United States—Biography. I. Title.
 ML420.E88N53 1997
 782.42166'092—dc20
 [B]   96-30621
                                                                      CIP
                                                                       MN

First St. Martin's Griffin Edition: March 1997

10 9 8 7 6 5 4 3 2 1

MELISSA ETHERIDGE

*I*NTRODUCTION

*R*ock 'n' roll is a boys' club. It always has been, from the moment Elvis sat down in Sun Studios on a recording break and began fooling around with "That's All Right, Mama." More than forty years have passed since that time, and they still don't want to let the girls in.

Anything women have wanted in rock they've had to fight for and claim for themselves; it's never been given to them. In that regard, music has run parallel with everyday life. Women in rock have had to be stronger, louder, and work harder to gain the respect they deserve. Pop music is a different matter. A female as a pop star has always been acceptable. After all, pop is a watered-down form, something easily digestible for the masses, without any grit or fiber. Much the same applies in folk music. There's not much aggression in introspective lyrics and a strummed acoustic guitar.

But crank up the volume, put a rough sandpaper edge on the voice, and the boys can become very scared indeed. They don't like the girls playing with their toys.

Which means that over the course of rock's story, only a handful of women have ever managed to break through to rock's hallowed higher ground.

There was Janis Joplin, of course. She could sing the blues, she could rock, she could live the life as well as any of her male counterparts. The music was in her soul, and it had to come out. To prove herself, though, she always had to go further. Drink, drugs, sex—she overindulged in them all, to the point of abuse. Whether she realized it or not, because she was a woman, there was always something to prove. And finally, tragically, it killed her.

After her, who was there? The boys had an endless series of heroes, the guitar slingers and singers, the noise merchants. On the female side it continued to look barren. Pat Benatar sounded good for a while; her music had plenty of MTV style but little substance, more fodder for the pop machine. Bonnie Raitt started out with a blues heart, but she ended up finding fame by mellowing out. The Wilson sisters of Heart could have had it—and maybe they did for a few moments in their early days—but they ended up choosing a path that emphasized commercial success.

If you were a girl and you wanted to rock, to turn the amp to ten and let it ring, the mainstream role models simply didn't exist.

Until Melissa Etheridge.

She's a woman who can give more than a little piece of her heart to every song. Someone to whom 100 percent was never quite enough. Passionate, unafraid of herself or of other people. Who likes the guitar to be as loud as the boys'. She's filled a need in music, a void, for the woman rock 'n' roller.

And she's done it in magnificent style. She's worked and worked, playing gig after gig to slowly build an audience over the years. She's honed her craft, her songs. Her career has blossomed into something spectacular; she can sell out stadiums all over the globe, and her records automatically sell in the millions.

For anyone, that would be a remarkable achievement. For a woman, it's incredible. For a woman who's an out lesbian, it's utterly unprecedented.

2

She defies every stereotype. Her songs speak to everybody, showing that whether heterosexual or gay, we share the same emotions—that at the heart of it all, it's passion and love that matter, not sexual orientation.

It's easy to bandy words like megastar and superstar around, to describe a level of success, of how many people know the name, buy the album, go to the concert. They're commercial signposts, and in a world ruled by the bottom line, they're important.

But Melissa offers something that goes beyond dollars and cents. She's a voice for women of all types, someone powerful and strong—someone who feels, and who has the ability to articulate those feelings. She's become a focal point for the lesbian community, someone who's been willing to stand up and be counted, who's been willing to come out and say exactly who she is, proudly, rather than stay in the closet. She's helped to give them a voice. And that's given her power, inside and beyond herself. There's nothing to hide any longer. She can be herself, with no reservations.

Perhaps the greatest thing she offers, though, is encouragement to a whole generation of girls, straight or lesbian. She's become a role model for so many of them. Punk and alternative have produced some very strong female performers, bands like 7 Year Bitch, Hole, and others. But it remains a minority music; there's a big difference between speaking up for yourself and confronting everything in the manner the Riot Grrl movement advocated. Melissa has shown that it's okay to sing about the place you're from, to sing about your passion, to play it loud, to *rock*. She speaks to the majority, not the margins.

It's really no surprise that her star has risen so high. There's been a need for someone like her for a long time, someone women could identify with, someone girls could look up to.

She didn't knock timidly on the clubhouse door and hope someone would open it and let her in. Instead, her music kicked it down and she strode inside as if she had as much right to be there as anybody else. And she did.

Like John Mellencamp, she's been called the sound of the heartland, the rock that Middle America can understand and identify with, where buzz words like "alternative" and the fleeting fashions of grunge hardly apply. Her music aims at a blue-collar audience, both men and women, where people work hard if there are any jobs to be had, and where music is a release. It's not a pose, an image. She *knows* that world. She grew up with it.

There's nothing fancy about it, no special trickery. Melissa has always dealt straight down the line, from the heart. It's about passion, about feeling something with every atom of your being until it almost devours you.

Her music has always cried out for stadiums. In an era when rock seemed to be downsizing, wanting to return to the clubs, her style seemed unfashionable. Even at their most intimate, the songs have a big sound, a full sound perfect for arenas. And these days she's become such a major star that those are the only venues able to accommodate all the people who want to see her. But whether it's a special event or one on an endless series of tour dates, it's a matter of faith for her to give all of herself at every show. If she doesn't, she feels she's not doing justice to herself, her material, and to the people who've paid to see her.

It's no surprise that her great heroes are Janis Joplin and Bruce Springsteen. Janis, after all, was the first to really break the gender barrier in rock. Melissa's voice has many of the same qualities: rough-edged, able to capture the spirit of a lyric, even if she arrived at it by a path that didn't include excess. There's even been talk of Melissa taking the title role in a film of Joplin's life, though whether that will happen remains to be seen.

Her reverence for Springsteen has a different foundation. When she was a teenager, his records showed her what it was possible to do with songs, how you could convey the hopes and dreams of working-class kids and make them into epics. What he did inspired her, gave her something to shoot for in her own work. And he, too, was someone who gave everything at a show, playing onstage for hours when he toured with his E Street Band, pushing every lyric home, making it count, and doing it all purely for the love of the music.

When she recorded her "Unplugged" show for MTV, and he appeared to duet with her on "Thunder Road," she said it was a highlight in her career.

But it was only one in a career that's seen so many. She's won two Grammys and been nominated for one more. She toured Germany when the Berlin Wall came down and played a spontaneous concert for freedom. Perhaps most important in the long run—at least to her—her music allowed her to meet the true love of her life, filmmaker Julie Cypher.

Being gay or lesbian in America isn't easy. There have been great strides toward acceptance, but intolerance remains rife throughout the country, its flames all too often fueled by the conservative, religious Right, who see homosexuality as a sin. There's still a long, long way to go. So it's not difficult to understand why Melissa was reluctant to "come out" for a long time.

Friends and many of her fans knew, or at least strongly suspected, her sexual orientation. In her private life it had never been a secret. But the public image had been a different thing since the beginning of her recording career. She had not denied anything, but neither was she about to volunteer the information.

She'd encouraged her friend k.d. lang to come out, and when lang did, the announcement didn't hurt her career at all. But k.d. appealed to an audience that was, by and large, different from Melissa's—more arty, more open and accepting in its views.

Eventually, though, the truth could no longer be kept a secret. And in 1993, at the Triangle Ball in Washington, D.C., a gay and lesbian event to celebrate the inauguration of Bill Clinton as President, it appeared.

It was an utterly spontaneous gesture, totally unplanned, from the heart, and the crowd went berserk.

Of course it was liberating. Now there didn't need to be any more secrets, words spoken off the record and kept hidden. Melissa could be herself, fully and completely. But there was also a great bravery in saying, "This is me, this is who I am." The gesture could easily have backfired.

Melissa enjoyed a much higher public profile than k.d. lang, who had come out publicly the previous year. She was an artist whose records sold in large quantities, whose voice was that of Middle America. Would those people accept a lesbian, or would she find herself on a downward spiral to oblivion, trapped inside the tag known as "cult artist" whose audience was made up of women and a few liberated men?

America not only accepted the real Melissa, it embraced her. When her next album, *Yes I Am*—the title often mistakenly taken solely as a confirmation of her sexuality—appeared, stores could barely keep it in stock. More than two years later it was still in the Billboard Top 200, with sales of over five million in the U.S. alone, making Melissa the first lesbian rock superstar—or, as she would more likely have stated, the first woman rock star who happened to be a lesbian.

"I'm sort of a gay success story," she told *The Advocate*, "a very inspirational one. What happened to me is exactly the opposite of what closeted people fear: They think they'll lose everything if they come out. This did not happen to me at all. In fact, everything came back tenfold."

Coming out more than freed her, it helped raise her to an entirely new level. With her down-to-earth, no-nonsense look and attitude, she essentially became America's favorite lesbian, someone who could quite easily have been the woman next door. The plaid shirts and jeans could have come from anyone's wardrobe, the no make-up style was basic.

One thing followed another. *Yes I Am* took off like a rocket. She made the cover of *Rolling Stone*, sold out tour after tour all over the globe. She and Julie became a very sensuous lesbian poster couple for PETA, People for the Ethical Treatment of Animals. She met the President. Every week, it seemed, was bringing something new and marvelous.

About the only thing not changed by her coming out was her music. It still had the raw power, the crackle of electricity. And still, as she'd always done, she addressed her songs to a genderless "You." She didn't need to do it any longer, of course, but it was her way. The emotions she expressed were human, not confined by sex. Keeping it like this included everybody.

That attitude, too, is typical of her polite, strong Midwestern upbringing. The lessons of childhood are thoroughly ingrained in her. There's no false front, no star trips around her.

Those are words spoken about many stars, to make them seem human and real. The difference is that with Melissa they also happen to be true. She's completely genuine; she's willing to take the time to talk to a fan and correct a misunderstanding over a lyric, or to encourage newcomers like Joan Osborne, who's toured with her several times.

With her partner, Julie, she's found happiness and contentment in her personal life. After meeting in 1988, when Julie was the assistant director shooting the video for "Bring Me Some Water," they've been together since 1990. In these days of come and go, that's a long time for *any* couple. The relationship had provided Melissa with a stable base, a family with which to surround herself.

Her star has risen, gradually at first, then at almost meteoric speed. From Leavenworth, Kansas, to the glitter of the Hollywood hills and socializing with the A-list of celebrities is a long, strange trip indeed. The old blue Chevrolet Impala that took her west is long gone, replaced by top-of-the-line Jaguars and BMWs. Still, at heart Melissa is midwestern steel, not fancy import glitz, the sound of sixties guitars playing power chords and singing choruses rather than the burble of a synthesizer or the mechanical beat of a drum machine. She's not the product of any technological wizardry or publicity machine.

Ultimately, that's why her appeal transcends any niche, why straights, gays, men, women, all buy her records and attend her concerts.

"Melissa's one of the leading women in rock because she exudes such pure, unadulterated honesty," David Geffen said. "She's a first-class rocker with a huge heart. She's as honest about her personal life as she is about her music. How can you not relate to sincerity?"

She may not be in Kansas anymore, but the spirit, the directness of the heartland remains in her music and her attitude. In the Midwest, roots run very deep. You can travel to the end of the earth and they're still inside you, maybe not pulling you back, but never quite letting you go, either. There's a strong sense of family attachments, of ties to the land. Melissa may owe musical debts to her major influences, but far more important in the story is where—and who—she came from. In order to begin to understand her, the value system that guides her, and the things that make her tick, that's the place you need to start. It made her, and she carries it with her every day.

*O*NE

*K*ansas is Middle America in more than name. Geographically it's the very center of the country, the heart of the heartland. Most of the communities in the state are small, towns that serve the farmers who try their best to make a living from the soil. Even today, when agribusiness on a massive scale has become the economic watchword, there are still plenty of spreads in Kansas that have been handed down through families for generations. Some do well for their owners, making them rich. For the majority, though, it's a tough life, long hours and hard work for a return that's not much more than subsistence. Still, they keep at it; it's the life they know, and persistence has always been part of the midwestern creed.

Leavenworth sits in the northeast corner of the state, almost at the Missouri border, above the Missouri River. Forty thousand people call it home. Kansas City lies some fifty miles to the south, accessible, but still far enough away to feel distant.

If Leavenworth is known for one thing, it's the federal penitentiary located there. Al Capone served his sentence in it, and during its history it's been home to any number of America's most famous criminals.

The town of Leavenworth is where Melissa Lou Etheridge was born on May 29, 1961. Her father, John, taught math and was the athletic director at the local high school, while her mother Elizabeth was employed by the U.S. Army at nearby Fort Leavenworth as a computer specialist.

The Etheridges already had one child, another daughter called Jennifer, who was four by the time Melissa was born, and now their family felt complete. It was a time when the American Dream still seemed a real possibility. A house, good, steady jobs, two kids—John and Elizabeth seemed to have it made.

Even living close to the prison wasn't a worry, as Melissa recalled in the *New York Times:* "Because the prisons were in the town, when the prisoners escaped they always went to the neighboring towns."

If life was good for John and Elizabeth, it hadn't always been that way. John was from the South. Born just before the Second World War, his childhood had been nomadic, following his own father, a migrant farmer, from place to place, job to job, often without money for essentials, let alone luxuries. His father was an alcoholic, using drink to block out the hardships of everyday life.

It would have been easy to remain trapped in the cycle of poverty, but John was determined not to let that happen to him. With help he was able to graduate from high school and go on to college, where he studied to become a teacher, settling finally in Kansas, where he met Elizabeth.

Her father, too, had been an alcoholic. Like John, she wanted to forget her past, abandon it as another country and start life anew.

"They did not have a drinking problem," Melissa said, "but they lived with that, and the emotional stigma was still passed down."

The couple married, bought a house, and settled in for a comfortable life. At least, it was comfortable on the surface. The

Etheridges weren't rich by any means, but hardly on the breadline, either. Emotionally, though, there was a real paucity of spirit.

"If I needed something, I had it," Melissa recalled in *Rolling Stone*. "But there was no feeling. There was no joy, there was no sadness or pain. And then if there was pain, it was just a nod." Communication wasn't at a premium. Many things that might have been explored went unsaid. Part of that undoubtedly stemmed from John and Elizabeth's unwillingness to delve too deeply into things, lest it bring up the past. Both John and Elizabeth, according to Melissa, had grown up with a lot of emotional turmoil, and their way of making sure it never returned was to simply avoid situations where it could occur. But that was also the way of the Midwest; feelings might be experienced, but they were hidden and rarely discussed.

"I was not shown as a child how to be angry; my parents kept their anger in, so I never grew up with examples of how to do that. I always thought, 'Well, that must mean that if I get angry, the world ends.' "

Despite this, there was love in the house. Melissa and Jennifer were both well cared for, even indulged, as much as the family budget allowed.

Almost from the first, Melissa was a ham, a performer. One of her first memories, from the time she was three, was of dancing for her parents and their friends, relishing the attention and the spotlight.

Given the time, it was almost inevitable that pop music would claim her. Jennifer, four years older, would leave the radio playing in the house.

"I was hooked on radio. It was the middle of the sixties, so we're talking the Beatles, Tommy James and the Shondells, Steppenwolf," Melissa recalled. But there was also the rhythm and blues, beaming out of Kansas City on small stations, and the more mainstream music her parents listened to: Neil Diamond, The Mamas & the Papas, Johnny Mathis. It all became part of her melting pot, and it wasn't long before she was doing the same as boys and girls all over America and forming a group with other kids on the block, using tennis rackets for guitars and pots and pans for drums. Melissa, naturally, played the tennis racket and sang, dreaming not of being a Beatle or a Stone, but an Archie. Specifically, Reggie.

"He was definitely the coolest. I wanted to be Reggie. He was dark, he was bad."

Surprisingly, though, she wasn't a natural singer.

"Early on, she didn't have a great voice," her mother remembered. "The music was in her; she was strumming the tennis racket from the time she was a toddler. I think some people are born with a singing voice, but I don't think she was. She just realized that was part of what she wanted to do, and she taught herself."

Soon it became quite apparent to John and Elizabeth that their younger daughter's obsession with music wasn't about to go away. Posing with a tennis racket had been fine for a while, but it didn't make noise; it wasn't the real thing. So, for Melissa's eighth birthday, they bought her a Harmony Stella six-string, and signed her up for guitar lessons with Don Raymond, a local jazz musician.

"He was real strict about timing. He tapped his foot really loud on an old wooden board. He's the reason I have really good rhythm," she said.

But jazz wasn't the kind of music she was looking to play at the time. What Melissa needed immediately was the basics, and as soon as she'd mastered those, she was happy, taking her guitar down to the basement and just playing for hours at a time. It became her way of dealing with her emotions and problems, taking them out on the steel strings, strumming and picking.

Within a couple of years she was writing, too. When she was ten, Melissa composed her first song, "Don't Let It Fly Away (It's Love)."

"I rhymed everything," she recalled years later, "love, above; bus with Gus."

The fact that she could do something like this, write a song like the ones she heard on the radio, was a complete revelation to her. Once she realized the possibilities that it raised, another girl was lost to music. She wanted to be a rock star. She *knew* she'd become a rock star, and went around telling everybody. It wasn't intended as a boast, just a simple statement of fact. Never mind that she didn't know of any female rock stars; that didn't matter. It was what she was going to do with her life.

"Melissa always had an amazing amount of self-confidence," Elizabeth Etheridge told *Rolling Stone*. "She never, ever said, '*If* I am able to do something in music.' It was always *when*.*"*

To anyone growing up in the sixties, music was a powerful force. But the ones it truly touched, those like Melissa, became enraptured by it.

Songwriting became the perfect way to deal with all the frustration and sorrow she felt. For a few minutes she could become the center of attention.

Even at age ten and eleven she knew that within her family, "underneath there was a lot going wrong. I didn't know how to tell them what I was feeling. That just wasn't done. But I could sit down and sing 'I'm so sad,' and they'd say, 'That's just marvelous.' "

Although she finished one song, more material didn't come flooding out. Another year would pass before the next one, "Lonely as a Child."

"It was really sad. It was about war in a land—because the Vietnam War was going on—and it was about a child in that land, and the mother was killed. It's just lonely as a child waiting for her mother to come home."

It was also the piece she performed when she appeared in public for the first time, entering a talent contest at the local mall, Leavenworth Plaza Tower.

She was nervous, but Melissa quickly discovered that she liked the stage, having people watch her and, more than that, being able to affect them with her words, her singing, and her playing.

Small towns build big dreams. At some point almost everyone

who grows up in one just wants to leave, to vanish into the wide world and never return to the stultifying atmosphere. For many the feeling passes, and they settle back to an ordered and happy life. But others know somehow that they're destined for something different, and that's the way it was with Melissa. Her experience of the world outside Leavenworth was limited to television and a few trips to Kansas City, but she already knew her future lay well beyond the heartland, in her fingers and her voice.

With the talent contest under her belt, she began spending more time than ever in the basement, learning new songs and continuing to write, including a piece for her grandmother, who'd recently passed away. For the most part, the material she composed was folky ballads, like "Lonely as a Child," which had brought such a good response at the mall.

"I think that's why my music was sad, and I could actually get a response from people. It was OK to make people cry, but it wasn't OK to cry, you know?"

Very soon her songs were getting positive responses all over Leavenworth and the surrounding small towns. The eleven-year-old with the long, straight hair and the big guitar would get up and entertain at teachers' conventions, churches, and nursing homes, her father driving her to and from the shows, standing quietly at the back while she entertained.

John Etheridge was a person who believed in politeness, in being *nice*, and doing unto others as you would have them do unto you. It was a trait he passed on to his younger daughter. She was a good girl, respectful of her elders, always remembering his advice to thank her audience—something she still does.

Melissa had discovered her own way of dealing with the family's lack of communication, channeling it into something creative and useful. Her older sister, though, didn't have that option. She became the girl who hung out and listened to loud music—which opened Melissa's ears to newer, louder bands like Humble Pie and Jethro Tull.

"She externalized it. She got angry. She was the bad kid. She always got in trouble," Melissa told *The Advocate.*

While John and Elizabeth were trying to deal with that, Melissa was expanding her horizons almost every day. At twelve she was becoming something of a veteran on the local music scene. Along with nursing homes and churches she now included bowling alleys, supermarket openings, Knights of Columbus Halls, and lounges on her circuit. She even made one appearance in a local jail. To many kids that would have been terrifying, but she reveled in the attention.

"Prisons have the most enthusiastic audiences," she explained to *Out.* "It's like playing for two thousand people who all want to be entertained." She added elsewhere, "I would go in and do a couple of my sad, original songs . . . that was fifteen hundred people. I was hooked."

Missy, as everyone had taken to calling her, just loved to play. It came naturally, and just felt right to her, to be up on stage, singing and playing. The hours up there, the hours in the basement, writing and practicing, fulfilled a need in her. And along the way she'd discovered something else about herself—she was a natural musician. Almost without effort, she was able to pick up the rudiments of almost every instrument she touched. So, in terrifyingly quick succession, she learned to play piano, drums, saxophone, and clarinet.

And, after trying a twelve-string guitar, she used the money she'd earned to buy herself one, just loving the fullness of sound it offered to accompany her voice.

What Melissa really needed, though, was a band to back her up and really let her belt the songs out, but Leavenworth was not exactly bulging with young rock bands willing to give a thirteen-year-old girl a chance.

It did, however, contain a country outfit called the Wranglers, and they were more than happy to accept the teenager on board to sing "Stand By Your Man" ("which is an amazing song just to holler" said Etheridge) and all the other Nashville favorites for the dances put on by Parents Without Partners and other organizations in the area.

Before too long, the Wranglers with Melissa Etheridge were beginning to win a bit of local reputation, and more bookings were coming in, including bars. By law Melissa shouldn't have been allowed in the bars, but that was where she'd be on Saturday night anyway, strumming a guitar and singing her heart out.

Her parents didn't drink, and if young Missy had ever wondered why not, when most of their friends did, those evenings provided the answer.

"I was watching these grown-ups drinking and getting sick and stuff. And I said, 'Hmm, that's disgusting.' "

It provided her with a very quick education in the ways of the adult world. But country music, although it was fun, didn't fill the creative urge that kept driving her onward. At home she was still spending most of her free time in the basement, working on her playing. Music became the center of her life, everything from Carole King and *Tapestry* to the Who's rock opera *Tommy*.

"I remember listening to *Exile on Main Street* and thinking 'What the hell is this?' . . . When I got to *Sgt. Pepper,* it totally blew my mind," Melissa told *Musician* magazine. Although the album had been out for several years by then, the power it held over an adolescent musician wasn't at all diminished. "One summer I listened to it every single day. It totally changed my life. I started realizing, words are important. Melodies are nice but words can make you think. You can get to people's bodies with music, and if you can make somebody think, then you've got their whole attention."

That was important to her. Her writing was becoming more and more proficient as she listened and learned more about her craft. As she entered those confused teenage years, it became a way to unleash her emotions, to express the things she couldn't really talk about at home.

Melissa's stint in the Wranglers didn't last long, but it taught her a great deal—how to work with a band, how to play to a noisy crowd out to be entertained, and how to project herself onstage. In high school she "hung out with the music and drama weirdos. We were very creative and very strange." But at Leavenworth High, where her father taught, she was also quite naturally well-behaved. Music class, in particular, enthralled her, and gave her an opportunity to demonstrate what she could do, maybe even to show off in front of the others a little bit. Lester Dalton, the teacher, was willing to indulge her.

"Melissa had a real gift for improvization and composition," he recalled. "She could come up with a song virtually at the spur of the moment."

The other kids were supportive. They already knew, because Missy had told them, that she was going to be a singer.

"I would play, and they'd say, 'God, you're good. You're going to make it. I'm going to say, "I knew you when." ' "

But that point still seemed a long, long way off. Melissa was taking the best that her hometown had to offer—"the Ramada Inn in Leavenworth, making twenty-five bucks a night"—but it wasn't going to make her famous. There were also some gigs with bands, anything and everything from Top 40 to country, just for the experience, but she knew there was something beckoning beyond all that.

Still, as long as what she was doing connected with music in some way, she was happy for the moment. Whether it was playing Dorothy in a school production of *The Wizard of Oz*, or being the entertainment at her own junior prom ("Commodores, Bee Gees, Fleetwood Mac. So unalternative."), every tiny little thing helped. Then she could go home and sing along at the top of her voice with someone whose music she'd recently discovered, and who was to prove a major catalyst in her writing: Bruce Springsteen.

"I used to go home from school, plug my eight-track tape in, listen to Bruce Springsteen, and dream," she'd tell the crowd at her "MTV Unplugged" performance.

He might have been singing about New Jersey, but even in Kansas Melissa knew exactly what he meant. His words—tales of getting out, breaking chains, driving forever without speed limits— spoke to her. And his band had all the adrenaline burst of great rock 'n' roll. "Born to Run," "Darkness at the Edge of Town"— she played them over and over. If any one person truly inspired Melissa, it was Bruce. One of the dreams she had while listening to his albums was of playing on the same stage with him one day. In 1978 that was pure fantasy: he was a star and she was sitting in her basement still trying to write songs that might someday live up to his. Seventeen years later, fantasy became reality when she asked him to join her for part of her "Unplugged" performance.

"It's like someone reached into your brain, plucked out your most secret fantasy, and gave it to you," she explained nervously.

One thing that passed her by in Springsteen's songs was the tales of young love. Between her music and schoolwork there simply wasn't time, even if she'd been especially interested. She did date occasionally, and when she did, she went out with boys. It wasn't just that she hadn't yet discovered she was a lesbian; the entire concept of lesbianism was foreign to her. It was more a case of relating to the individual rather than the gender.

"I was sixteen years old the last time I dated a man," she told *The Advocate.* The other girls at school might have been obsessed with boys, but Missy just didn't see the attraction. Like everybody, she experienced a few crushes, but nothing she wanted to follow through on.

By the time she turned seventeen, she'd become a "strange, butch guitar player." She'd also realized where her sexuality lay, beginning a relationship with a girlfriend. "I kiss my first girl, and fireworks go off, and music is playing. And then it's just . . . clear."

It was a revelation to her, and suddenly she understood the giddy emotions and sensations of love that everyone else had been feeling.

At school a lot of people seemed to guess about her orientation.

Graffiti like "Missy is a Lezzie" began to appear on the bathroom walls. Melissa was different from all the others. She stood out, and that made her a target. But the fact that she could get up and perform, write songs to let her feelings go, helped her cope with it. It also gave her some grudging respect from her peers. So, in the long run, she really didn't care what they wrote on the walls. Her time in Leavenworth was running out. She knew she'd be leaving; let them think what they wanted.

One thing she did, however, was come out to her father. She'd always felt closer to him than to her mother. He was the one who drove her to the endless series of gigs all over northeast Kansas, the one who'd offered her an example of how to live and treat people by the way he intereacted with his students. Even if his background had left him emotionally stunted, Melissa wanted to be honest with him. She wanted to break the pattern of noncommunication.

It wasn't easy. Coming out can be traumatic enough for an adult. For a teenager, going through a terribly confusing time anyway, to come out to her dad had to be one of the toughest things she'd ever done. But she sat down with him and talked, building up the conversation until he understood she was going to say something very important.

"And I finally said, 'I'm a homosexual.' And he said, 'Is that it?' He thought it was just going to be something really terrible."

John Etheridge accepted his daughter's admission quite calmly. But Melissa would be twenty-three before she could sit down and talk about her lesbianism with her mother. Elizabeth had known for quite a while—John hadn't been asked to keep it a secret—but the topic had remained unspoken and the feelings unresolved, largely because of Melissa's "relationship with my mother. It was strained as a child, and I think that adds to my attraction to women. It's about what I didn't get as a child; that female energy I crave. But I think I had to be born [a lesbian] first."

Once she'd sorted out who she was and what she was, life began to make a lot more sense. Still, this was the late 1970s, and Kansas wasn't full of out lesbians to offer her any examples. The only thing she could do was what came naturally, what felt right. "It's bad enough being straight and dealing with adolescent sexuality," she said. "It was very hard, very lonely."

All-consuming as this seemed, it had to coexist with her music. There were regular gigs to play, practicing to be done, and plenty of new songs just waiting to be written. A new life with a girlfriend had to happen in moments stolen from that, finding a balance between the two. And just because Melissa was out to her father and the kids at school thought they knew what she was didn't mean the relationship could be open. It was still the love that dare not speak its name.

Inside it felt right to her, so she knew it couldn't be wrong, but she did keep it quiet. The songs she wrote couldn't be addressed to a woman. So she began writing to someone genderless. *She* knew she was writing to, and about, women, but her audiences never suspected that the original material interspersed with their favorites had so many undertones.

There was, of course, no thought about coming out publicly. This was still the Midwest, and perilously close to the Bible Belt. A lot of people still saw homosexuality as a sin; a number of states had laws against homosexual acts in the statute books. It might have been the 1970s, but enlightenment for many remained beyond the horizon.

Melissa knew that Kansas held no future for her. Once she'd graduated from high school, she planned to leave. Playing hotel lounges, nursing homes, the circuit she'd put together for herself, was fine for a kid. The experience had been invaluable. But it wasn't going to help her music develop. It didn't expose her to all the other influences she needed, the loud blast of rock 'n' roll, the interaction with other musicians who could stimulate her. It had been a great place to start out, but it had given her everything she could use. It was time to begin thinking about fresh challenges, in a place where she could more openly be herself, where being that strange, butch guitar player was acceptable.

She was ready to try her wings. After all, there was a whole world out there to be conquered by her music. But her parents wanted her to go through more formal musical training, and that meant college.

"I didn't want to go to college, but I wanted to leave Leavenworth. So I thought, 'OK, maybe I'll go to a music college. This could be a compromise.' "

Initially they suggested the big schools like Juilliard and Eastman, but Melissa wasn't having any of that. Granted, she could play a number of instruments quite well. The problem was that these schools were immersed in tradition. Neither offered a guitar major, which was what she really wanted. Instead she'd have been forced to major in voice, "and can you hear me singing opera?"

Melissa countered it with another suggestion: Berklee College of Music, in Boston. The emphasis was different there, far more on the contemporary, and it welcomed good guitarists. Since it *was* a college, and it had good credentials, John and Elizabeth gave in and let her apply.

Meanwhile she continued to play her circuit, writing songs, and seeing her girlfriend as time and circumstances allowed. There was always something that needed to be done.

By now Melissa was chafing to be away from Leavenworth, from Kansas, from the Midwest. When the acceptance letter came from Berklee she could begin to count the days to leaving.

What she didn't realize then was how much of it she'd be taking along with her. The small-town sensibility of Leavenworth had shaped her values, her work ethic. She knew to treat people the way she'd like to be treated, to give her job—her music—everything she could, every time. It was hardly a surly, dismissive rock 'n' roll attitude she was carrying, but that was all to the good. Her way would carry her much further. Like her hero, Bruce Springsteen, she looked at life from a blue-collar perspective, not so much an observer as a participant.

In Leavenworth the biggest employer was the Hallmark factory, making greeting cards and candles. As graduation rolled around and the class of '79 made their plans, some of them were hearing the call of the plant. It was steady work, secure, well paid. That was what they wanted, a future all mapped out for them. They could work, party on the weekends for a couple of years, then go steady, marry, and have families. Take a vacation every year in the Ozarks or somewhere farther afield. Retire at sixty-five and enjoy life.

To Melissa that was hardly better than being a prisoner in the federal penitentiary down the block from her house. Growing up in a small town had been fine. But as soon as the chance to escape came, she needed to take it. When she was young, the family had occasionally taken the trip to Kansas City for home and garden shows. Back then the lights of the city, its noise and bustle, had appealed to the girl. It was somewhere she wanted to be, to feel herself surrounded by its energy. She'd never forgotten it.

The summer passed slowly. Everyone she'd known in school gradually took on other, more adult lives. The days were hot and sticky and endless. She spent her time in the basement, working on her guitar technique, writing some new songs. Although she couldn't see it closely, the image of Boston and Berklee grew stronger in her mind. A place where no one would be writing "Missy is a Lezzie" on the wall, because they wouldn't care. Where she could be herself, and Missy and Melissa Lou could vanish, to be replaced forever by just Melissa.

While she had high hopes for the things she could learn about music at college, she knew that college wasn't an end in itself. It was a tool to help her along the way. Deep inside she understood that her future was in rock 'n' roll. It had given her so much while she was growing up. It had comforted her, taken her places. And now she was ready to start giving something back.

July and August ticked by. Labor Day came and went, the air filled with the smell of family barbecues. John Etheridge returned to the high school for a new year of teaching. All Melissa had to do was pack. Her clothes were selected, her records, her guitar always ready to travel in its hard-shell case.

Finally it was time to leave, to cram everything she was taking into the family car, kiss her mother good-bye, and let her father drive her to the airport in Kansas City. After all the anticipation and the idea that leaving home made her an adult, she felt like a little kid again, passing through the streets of Leavenworth, then watching the town disappear in the rear view mirror—just like something from a Springsteen song.

The airport bustled with activity. At the gate, people sat, casually reading magazines or glancing out the window. This was the point of no return. As soon as that plane took off, Melissa was beginning a new life.

When the boarding call came, she found her seat and settled in. The noise of the takeoff was loud. Climbing into the sky, she found herself looking back, at the scenery, at her life, until Kansas became just a memory below the clouds.

She had plenty of dreams to sustain her during the flight, hopes for everything the future might hold. She wanted the big time, and she was willing to work hard for it. At home everyone had told her she had the talent to make it. In Boston, in the big city, she'd begin to find out if that was really true.

_T_wo

_B_y everything Melissa had experienced, Boston wasn't just a large city, it was a metropolis. Because Boston was home to a number of universities and colleges, a multitude of students swelled the already large local population. There were street musicians, buskers, on busy corners or in the subways, playing their guitars and singing for spare change. Most were mediocre at best, but a few were good, really talented.

It was a place to open her mind.

Boston also had a strong lesbian scene. It was a place where they could be open, and more accepted in the liberal air that blew down from the campuses. In among the many small businesses eager to cater to the young population were women's bookshops, their shelves stocked with feminist and lesbian literature.

And there were the lesbian bars. These days most cities of any size have at least one, usually more. To Melissa, though, fresh from the Midwest and still quite naive, they were a revelation. Going into one was like entering a whole new world.

"I was like 'My God, look at all these people.' " she recalled. "And they're all dancing and having fun."

Perhaps for the first time she understood that it was possible to be open about the way she felt, rather than having to hide it or, at best, keep it quiet.

"I met all these gay women. I wasn't alone. There were people just like me."

In Boston she was surrounded by more than a few women like herself. After Leavenworth it had to feel very comforting.

Gradually she became acclimated to the city. What had seemed both fascinating and frightening at first slowly became part of the everyday—the coffee shops where she was able to see other singers perform, the bars and odd little stores. The city was a great education in life for a midwestern girl.

But after the politeness and slow pace of a small town, Boston was certainly fast and rude. Drivers would get into fistfights over parking spaces. Outside of a circle of friends, no one would smile and say "Good morning" on the street. The small courtesies, the things Melissa had grown up taking for granted, didn't exist there, and it was difficult to keep them going in herself.

But she was there to study, and that had to be her focus—not the nightlife, not socializing, although they were impossible to ignore. There were always so many things going on, places to go, people to see.

At school she found herself surrounded by plenty of talented musicians. Back in Leavenworth her talent had made her stand out; the ability to write songs and play several instruments had set her apart. At Berklee College of Music all that changed. Everyone was good there; they had to be, just to get in. Some were phenomenally gifted on their instruments, with guitar a particular favorite. Walking the halls, she could hear fingers ripping easily through complex runs of notes at any time of the day.

Although Berklee attracted people who were more interested in rock 'n' roll than the classics, it was not an easy option; quite the opposite. It wanted its graduates to be as well trained as any in the world. The classes and courses were rigorous, the standards high. The school expected, and demanded, a great deal of work from its students.

Unfortunately, that was something Melissa was unable to do. "I just couldn't apply myself," she explained in *Michigan Monthly Music Revue.* "I was too caught up in the dream of being a rock star rather than being 'a musician.' The energy you spend studying for that, I would rather spend looking for jobs singing in bars and restaurants."

That, after all, was what she knew how to do. She was young enough to think that the dream of stardom would carry her, but realistic enough to know that she still had to make a living. From her experience, she understood that restaurants and bars offered a solid, if unspectacular, living, a grounding in entertaining people, which was, after all, the bottom line of the business.

Dreams and ambitions and academia clashed inside her. It wasn't as if she was cutting classes or ignoring her work. She was doing everything that was asked of her. But her heart simply wasn't in it. As it was, college had been a compromise, something she'd done more to please her parents than herself. The longer she stayed, the more she discovered that it wasn't what she wanted or needed in her life. Classrooms were no substitute for audiences.

Near the end of her second semester, before she could even complete a whole year, Melissa dropped out of school.

"Part of me wishes I had stayed longer so that I would be a more accomplished musician," she admitted years later. "I would certainly play guitar better. But I didn't have the patience."

There was a whole world waiting, and she was ready to go out and grab her share. It's ironic, then, that in the brochures Berklee sends prospective students, Melissa's picture is proudly displayed alongside the other alumni, even though she never came close to graduating.

It's always easy to say in hindsight that things turned out for the best, but part of Melissa's appeal has always been the rawness, not just of her voice, but of her talent. It's direct, spontaneous, and utterly honest. Four years of study, of making her think about her work instead of just feeling it, might well have left her a different person. She probably would have ended up a better technical musician, but more formal training might also have affected her writing style. It might have become more polished and considered, and almost certainly it would have ground down the rough edges that have always made her stand out. In the trade-off of education and career, in the long run she ended up gaining far more than she lost. And constant practice has helped keep her instrumental skills sharp.

Still, the decision to leave Berklee wasn't easy. It was bound to be a source of disappointment to her parents; they were the ones who'd wanted her to get a solid education that would have left her in a position to teach music when this rock 'n' roll bug had worked its way through her system. Melissa had tried, and found that her head was too full of the future to be able to concentrate on the present. Finally, it had to be up to her. She was the one who knew whether it was working or not.

Of course, John and Elizabeth Etheridge wondered what Melissa would do if she quit school, and she had the answer to that—she'd *be* a musician, instead of studying to become one. Didn't she already have years of experience under her belt, talking to people, getting gigs, playing in almost every type of situation? She was convinced she could make a living from music, and that seemed the important thing, to be doing it instead of talking about it. She'd done it in Leavenworth, and she believed she could do it in Boston. That would be the foundation she could build on and work toward putting out her own albums, achieving her own ambition of being a rock 'n' roll star.

So she left Berklee, moved into an apartment, and began making the rounds of lounges, coffeehouses, and clubs, anywhere that featured live music. What she quickly discovered was that musically, Boston was nothing like Kansas. The city was full of guitarists and singers, all of whom seemed to have dreams like hers. Boston drew hopefuls from around the country. In the clubs, you were lucky if you could get a gig once a month, playing a short set well down the bill, before the crowds even arrived to see the headliners. The coffeehouses weren't much better. They'd been operating for decades, and had seen plenty of talent go through—names like Joan Baez and Bonnie Raitt—when they were still unknowns. Every amateur musician who could strum a guitar and pen a lyric was out there, trying to be discovered.

The real world, Melissa quickly found out, could be harsh. Spending money was easy. Every day there was cash going out for groceries, rent, utilities, but very little was coming in. She wanted to stay in Boston. The place seemed full of opportunity. Not only did it promise career possibilities, but in the bars she could be around women like herself, and that was truly liberating. To stay, though, she needed money. She even tried to emulate the street musicians she'd seen when she arrived, setting up in Park Place subway station, guitar case open in front of her, going through her repertoire. But playing for quarters, dimes, and the occasional dollars just wasn't going to make it. Finally she made what was really a momentous decision: She was going to get a job.

It was the first, and it would be the last time she'd work outside music. Not that she was giving it up—whatever work she found, it had to be something that would give her the time to play, so she could still hit those coffeehouses and clubs when the opportunity arose.

Despite the competition even for regular jobs in Boston, she found something. At five feet three inches, Melissa might have seemed too small to be a security guard, but that was exactly what she became, working her shift at Deaconess Hospital. It was only part-time work, but enough to help her survive and let her pursue what was really in her heart. Wearing a uniform and patroling the halls paid her bills, but she knew she couldn't do it for too long. What she really needed was to be making a living from her music. As 1980 became 1981 the situation hadn't improved. Melissa was still working at the hospital and finding gigs wherever she could, spending more time talking to bookers and auditioning than playing for the public. After months of making little headway, she was starting to think that maybe Boston really wasn't the place for her. New Wave, the pop offspring of punk, had taken over everything. No one was interested in a woman who played straight-ahead rock 'n' roll.

"New Wave was the sound," she explained. "There were bands like the Rings, the Cars . . . I didn't feel like I fit."

Some bands were coming out of Boston with recording contracts. The Cars had become a major band. For most, though, playing in the city seemed to be an end in itself, possibly a dead end. The record companies didn't have offices there; they were based in New York and Los Angeles. Melissa had just gone through enough to realize that if she was going to try her luck in one of those two cities, she needed either money or contacts. With all the labels myopically focused on what was happening now, money would be easier to come by.

The problem was that it meant leaving Boston, and Melissa wasn't a quitter by nature. She'd dropped out of Berklee not because she couldn't do the work, but because it wasn't the right place for her. Moving away from Boston before she'd made her mark almost seemed like failure. But in the long run, it would help her career, push her farther along the path she wanted to walk. She handed in her notice at the hospital.

Then she called her parents to tell them she was moving home.

It was a huge decision to make, but to Melissa it made a lot of sense. She'd had no problems finding work as a musician in Kansas before, and now she was better, tougher. She'd work there for a while, save her money, and then give her music a real push. She'd go to Los Angeles, where dreams came true every day.

Back in Leavenworth, little seemed to have changed. Compared to Boston, the place seemed quiet and orderly. The people were polite and friendly, the same faces Melissa had been seeing all her life. She hadn't come back to lick her wounds after not making it in the city. Although there was a love of the Midwest deep inside her, she was here to work hard, live cheaply, save money, and try again. No more laboring as a security guard, or any other minimum wage job to keep body and soul together. From now on it had to be music, all the way.

The circuit she'd played through school had been fine then, when she was still a kid. Melissa was a woman now, twenty years old, and she needed something more constant and better paying, a place where she could work alone.

In the end, that meant one thing: Kansas City. Less than an hour's drive from her parents' house, it was an easy enough commute, and it was a city with a nightlife, where a singer and guitarist could find work. The Granada Royale Hotel had a bar that needed live music, and Melissa made herself fit the bill for the Lavaranda Lounge.

The job wasn't rock 'n' roll, not even her own material, but it put money in her pocket, fairly good money. After Boston, it also was a relief to have a regular gig. So what if she was playing Barry Manilow, Lionel Ritchie, and Fleetwood Mac, all the easy listening favorites? It was experience, and it was music. This was a stopping-off point. There would be time for her own songs later.

It was easy work. Every evening she'd drive down to the city, sing and play for the drinkers. When she was finished, she'd pack up her equipment and go to one of the gay bars in Kansas City.

In Boston she'd been able to be herself, and that was wonderful. Back home she had to be more circumspect, more closeted, and it left her lonely. The bars were her distraction. To give herself something to do while she sat in them, Melissa briefly took up smoking.

"In my experience the only place you could meet other gay people was in a bar," she explained in *Rolling Stone*. "And the worst thing in the world is to sit in a bar alone, right? So a cigarette could be your best friend." But as soon as smoking began to affect her voice, Melissa quit. "I went 'OK, no matter how lonely I am, I have to sing.' "

She was willing to live with the loneliness, as hard as it was. She had a goal, a dream, and nothing was going to deter her from it. Anything else came a distant second.

Night after night she played for the traveling businessmen at the Lavaranda Lounge, sometimes throwing in one or two of her own mellower pieces as she became more used to the place. The nights weren't too bad. At least she had something to do, work, then perhaps a trip to a gay bar if she wasn't too exhausted.

The days were a different matter. When she'd lived in Leavenworth before, she'd still been in school. Her time had been programmed for her. Now the daylight hours were free, and there was little to fill them. The people she'd known were all working, which left her to her own devices. And since she didn't have a car of her own—she used her father's vehicle in the evening—she was stuck in town.

At least she still had her parents' basement, where she could play and write the material that really moved her. It was an antidote to all the pap that brought in the cash—loud, hard rock 'n' roll, nothing more or less.

Melissa was frustrated, there was no doubt about that. Having escaped the Midwest once and tasted all the possibilities, she was eager to get out again, but this time she was determined to wait until she could do it right. It was a struggle to be the quiet entertainment in the evening, having little time to look for a girlfriend, having to submerge her real personality every day. Still, she managed to do it, and it was an important lesson for her. She could do what it took, and she could stick to it. She could make a living from her music, even if it wasn't in the way she'd hoped. She was a survivor.

As time passed, her savings account kept growing. When 1982 arrived in the middle of a typical Kansas winter, all snow and cold, Melissa still made it to the Granada Royale Hotel every night. She'd fallen into a routine. Sooner or later she'd have to break it and make her great leap into the unknown. For now, however, this worked. Perched on a stool in the corner with her guitar, or sitting at the grand piano, her small body almost hidden by the instrument, she *made* it work.

Constant playing, and the challenge of learning new material—the softer Top 40 hits—improved her technique. Maybe not as much as another few years at Berklee would have, but her playing continued to improve. She grew to understand the subtleties of song construction, and on some level it all went into the thing she really cared about—her own music.

That remained the driving force. The songs still poured out of her, helping her get rid of all her frustration and desires. When she played she could be herself, and enjoy some sort of catharsis.

As her twenty-first birthday approached, Melissa knew it was time to start putting her plans into action. The longer she delayed, the less likely that anything would happen, and the stultifying atmosphere of Kansas would swallow her.

The first thing she needed was a car: a big car to transport all her stuff to the west coast, and a cool car that she'd feel happy driving. After looking around she found the perfect one, a 1964 Chevrolet Impala, blue, in good mechanical condition. This was the car she'd mention years later in the song "Nowhere to Go" on *Your Little Secret*, one of her most autobiographical pieces, about the closeness of small towns and the need to sneak away for love.

The car was not too expensive, leaving her money to survive for those first few months following her move, until she could land a regular gig or a record deal.

For her, as for so many around the country, California, and Los Angeles in particular, remained a mythic place. For several generations, almost since the Gold Rush, it had seemed like the state where riches could be had for the taking. After L.A. became the center of the entertainment industries, stories like that of Lana Turner being "discovered" in a drug store only fueled the desires of the young to make their way out there. It remained the land of opportunity.

At the beginning of May Melissa handed in her notice at the Lavaranda Lounge. She had a sense of anticipation, a feeling that she was doing the right thing in taking this chance. Realistically she knew she had good songs, a good voice. But was the world ready for a woman rock 'n' roller who played guitar and wrote her own material? That was what she'd have to find out. At least she had the skill, the experience, and the repertoire, to play the lounges and bars out there. After all, how hard could it be to get a gig like that?

At home she sorted through her clothes and other possessions, deciding what to take and what to leave, paring down to the basics that would fit in the car. She'd done this only a couple of years before, heading out to Berklee. This time it was different; the West Coast would be a make-it-or-break-it-time. She wanted to make a living from her music. She believed she could. She was going to give it everything she had. And she was going to make it all happen for herself.

"I'd always had this vision of L.A.: that a girl with a guitar could go there, that you could be a Fleetwood Mac. And I knew that L.A. was where the record companies were. This was where I was going to get signed."

It was the belief of the Midwest in the infinite possibilities of the West Coast. Out there anything could happen, and if you had talent, then you'd end up a star. Most didn't, but that didn't stop more people arriving every single day of the year.

And now Melissa was making her preparations to join them. On May 28, 1982, she packed the car, cramming the backseat and the trunk. The gas tank was full, the engine had been checked over, there was plenty of air in the spare tire and the jack worked easily. She was ready for the road.

The following day she turned twenty-one. There wasn't a big celebration. Instead Melissa stowed a few final things in the glove compartment and said good-bye to her parents. It was a new year, a new beginning. The future was wide open ahead of her. She turned the key, pulled out of the driveway, drove down the streets she knew all too well, then along the road to Kansas City she'd taken too many times in the last year, then finding the Interstate, hitting the gas pedal, and heading west.

The flatlands and ripening wheat gave way to desert scenery as she moved through New Mexico. By the time she reached Arizona the summer heat had become intense. But every mile was bringing the dream nearer. Finally she crossed the California state line, and a few hours later Los Angeles shimmered on the horizon. She'd arrived.

*T*HREE

*S*he'd made it all the way to the Golden State, but that didn't mean Melissa would find smooth sailing from now on. The magnet that drew so many to Los Angeles meant that the competition for work was tremendous.

She also arrived just as heavy metal music was making a resurgence in the clubs. It was proving very popular, filling places night after night, which meant, not surprisingly, that it was all the owners wanted to book.

"I got here in '82 and it was right at the beginning of Guns N' Roses. There was no place for a woman with an acoustic guitar, though I was playing rock 'n' roll. Even the Troubadour was heavy metal. I was very disappointed and very scared."

To the masses, how could a woman alone, playing a twelve-string, compare with the crunch of Marshall amps turned all the way to ten and the thud of drums? Next to all that she sounded like a delicate folk singer. Bands were what people wanted, and that wasn't the way Melissa performed.

Even if she had been able to find gigs in the rock clubs, she still wouldn't have been able to make a living from her music.

"You can't play and make money in L.A.," she told *Interview*. "There are so many musicians who are willing to play for free, or even pay to play, that I couldn't make a living."

Time and again she made the rounds of every venue in the city that advertised live music. It didn't even matter what *type* of music; she knew she could play anything and everything. She had quickly abandoned dreams of overnight stardom once she saw the reality of the situation. But before she'd left Kansas she'd vowed to herself that she'd only live off her music—no more security guard jobs, or anything similar—and she was going to do everything she could to make sure that happened.

Melissa auditioned at every place that would let her, but the pickings were slim. Lounges wanted something more sophisticated than a guitar, bars wanted bands, and as for all the other places, she didn't seem to fit there, either. She even failed, again and again, to secure an audition at a Hollywood health food restaurant called the Natural Fudge Company.

After a few months her money was beginning to run out, and she was willing to compromise about what constituted making a living from her music. She tried out as a singing waitress.

"It was at a place called the Great American Burger Co., I think," was how she recalled the incident. "It was a family wedding. This little girl looked at me and stuck out her tongue."

That wasn't what she had planned for her life. It wasn't the reason she'd spent hours in the basement writing songs and practicing guitar. It had absolutely nothing to do with why she'd moved west. And singing while serving food at family weddings wasn't going to advance her career a bit. Maybe what she had was a midwestern thing that just wouldn't play on the coasts.

She was close to broke—"I hocked my typewriter"—lonely, and feeling adrift in Los Angeles. As they had in Boston, the gay and lesbian bars offered a place for solace and companionship.

A number of the bars were located in Long Beach, a community south of L.A. In one of the women's bars there, the Executive Suite, Melissa noticed a piano in the corner.

"And I said, 'Do you have live music?' 'Now and then,' they said. And I said, 'Can I come and audition? I'll come on Sunday.'"

That Sunday, when Melissa sat down with her guitar, the bar was busy. She gave it everything she had, knowing this was her big chance, maybe even her last chance. She had a sympathetic audience and a chance to really show what she could do, mixing her own songs in with the covers. To be performing again, getting the feedback and excitement of a crowd, felt wonderful.

It went well. She was "a huge hit."

"And I got the job. I played five nights a week before the disco."

Finally, after months of trying, she was settled into a job, playing music in a place that was perfect for her, part of a circuit among the women's bars that she'd never known existed. Life was beginning to look up. She could relax a little, and take the time to enjoy life. The fact that most of the music she'd be playing was by other people didn't bother her at all.

"I made a conscious decision not to have a day job," she explained, "which meant I had to sing other people's music four or five nights a week. And I'm glad I made that decision. I learned a lot about performing."

One of her most important discoveries in California was the music of Janis Joplin, whom she'd never really heard before—an irony, given the similarities in their voices.

"I listened only to Janis for three months," Melissa recalled in *Musician.* "When I started catching her old stuff, like 'Piece of My Heart,' that was it for me. I started singing it in the bars and people just went nuts."

What she found in the way Joplin tackled a song was something she wanted to be able to bring out of herself, "the passion, in going heavy and screaming and hollering and putting it all out. That was the influence she had on me."

But really, there was more. Janis had been the first female rock star, indeed more or less the only one who had found equal stature with the men. That made her someone to look up to in Melissa's eyes. Janis had achieved the stature Melissa ultimately wanted.

One thing Melissa didn't want was to pay the same price. She was very much a professional; she'd been playing in bars for eight years, and had seen her share of drunks. It wasn't a future she wanted for herself.

"Sure, I went through some wild periods," she admitted. "I'd say my early twenties were pretty crazy. But I was always conscious in the craziness. I mean, I got messed up, absolutely. But I was always conscious and aware of putting on a good show."

The craziness wasn't drink and drugs—at most, Melissa has never been more than a light social drinker—but the chance to indulge herself sexually. After having to be very closeted in Kansas, she was eager to take advantage of all the opportunities now offered, and she did, in a series of brief relationships.

Work came well ahead of any fun, however. Not just performing, where she was making good money for the first time in her life, but also writing, as she'd always done. Along with the Joan Armatrading, Fleetwood Mac, and other covers, she began cautiously playing her own material onstage, and it got as good a reception as the better-known songs.

"People who were interested started requesting my own stuff. It was really the breeding ground for the confidence in my music," she said.

Her ability was growing, her writing was improving, and she was making a decent living. But the Long Beach bar scene wasn't bringing her any nearer to record companies or the kind of rock 'n' roll stardom that remained her ultimate goal. It was a women's scene, very insular, and most of the label executives were men who'd be highly unlikely to drop in to the Executive Lounge for a quiet drink after work.

What she needed was contacts. She was still an outsider in California. One thing she'd quickly learned was that in the music business, indeed in almost everything, it wasn't what you knew that counted, but who you knew.

Fate, however, was waiting to help her out. Regularly, women's teams—softball, soccer, any kind of sport—would come into the bar after their games to unwind, celebrate, or commiserate. Not all of them were lesbians. The bar was simply a place where they could relax and have fun, without being constantly hassled by men.

One of the soccer teams included a woman married to a man in the music business. Every time she was in the Executive Lounge she'd hear Melissa, who'd been performing there for almost a year now, and was impressed. Finally she asked for a tape that she could pass on. Melissa didn't have one available, but she made sure that soon changed, going into a cheap studio and cutting a solo recording of her own songs.

"He heard the tape: 'Sure, that's pretty good.' Came down to the bar to hear me and has been my manager [since]: Bill Leopold."

Bill had been around the music industry for a long time—he'd managed the group Bread in the 1970s—and he knew a lot of people at record labels. He became the first person in the business to believe in Melissa, who was willing to do what he could to help her career. It had only been eleven years since her first appearance, and finally she was on her way.

It was a start, but nothing more than that. She was still playing five nights a week at the Executive Lounge, although before too long she'd move to another bar, the Que Sera Sera. The music was still mostly covers, with a few of her originals added here and there. One thing it definitely wasn't was out-and-out rock 'n' roll, although she was doing her best to make it so. Her confidence had grown, and she'd become much more than a musical wallflower at the bar.

"I had gone from a quiet sort of 'Hey, I'm just here in the corner and you don't have to listen to me' thing to standing up and doing a show, playing rock with an acoustic guitar and making people listen."

She decided to try her luck at some of the women's music festivals that took place during the summer. Along with relatively well-known performers like Holly Near, who'd managed to break through to the national consciousness in a small way, the bill was full of performers like Melissa—strong but unknown. After time on the bar scene, which she described as "very hard-edged," she found the festivals to be something of a revelation, and not an especially welcome one. The audience was comprised of a different part of the lesbian community, which tended not to visit bars, and who tended toward early feelings of political correctness.

In an interview published in *The Advocate*, she said: "I remember doing a monologue once where I talked about being with a girl and having her leave me and what I went through—gaining ten pounds and stuff like that. Well, after the concert I literally had to hold off all these women who were saying that the songs I sang were all about abuse and that the comment I had made about being ten pounds overweight was terrible and that they were going to come and string me up. It was my first PC call, you know. I realized, 'Oh, there's so many things I have to be aware of.' . . . I was left there saying 'What? What did I do? It was always fun in the bars.' Sometimes it's hard to be a lesbian."

It left her realizing that her best option remained getting a record deal with a major company. Leopold went to work on her behalf to make Melissa's rock dreams come true. He played her tape for people in the artist and repertoire (A & R) departments at a number of labels, which was enough to convince them to come and see what she could do live.

What they saw impressed them all. It was obvious that Melissa had the presence and the personality to command attention. She was perfectly at home on a stage, working an audience.

They were definitely interested, but time and again that was as far as it went. Melissa came close to being signed by Capitol, A&M, Warner Brothers, and EMI. Over three years they all talked to Leopold, and saw Melissa perform. But something kept holding them back.

Could it have been the fact that she was playing in a primarily lesbian bar? Melissa didn't want to think that.

"I chose to believe that everyone who came down just didn't hear a hit single. Period."

Whatever the real reason was, it became an extremely frustrating period for her. There would be the rising pitch of excitement in talking to the label, the performance that she knew was good, followed by the inevitable letdown as the fascination waned and another possibility bit the dust. She was coming closer, thanks to Leopold, and she knew that sooner or later, something would happen. But she had her hopes raised and shattered so many times that she could only have wondered when, finally, it would all be over.

The answer was: not for a long time. It would be 1986 before things really started to break, almost four years after she'd begun playing the bars.

In the meantime, at least she was making a comfortable living, enough so she didn't have to watch every cent. In 1984 Elizabeth Etheridge had made a trip to the West Coast to see how her daughter was getting along. Since Melissa had become an adult, the two hadn't spent much time alone together, so the visit gave them the opportunity to talk properly. It also gave Melissa the chance to come out to her mother, to explain who she really was.

Elizabeth already knew that her daughter was a lesbian. But knowing it and hearing it directly from Melissa were two different things.

For Elizabeth Etheridge, it was all confusing at first.

"I didn't quite know how to deal with it," she admitted. But over the course of her visit, she was able to finally come to terms with Melissa's sexuality. "I saw how lovely her friends were and how happy she was, and that's always been my main concern."

After all the lack of communication Melissa had felt during her childhood, and her need for her mother's approval, it was a good, truthful place to begin building bridges.

"We finally started coming back together and learning about each other and becoming friends, it was great. 'Whatever, as long as you're happy.' " The visit was a step toward sorting out and working through the past. Things were improving for Melissa.

Around this time she even made a foray into acting with a very brief walk-on appearance in the short-lived CBS television series *I Had Three Wives*, starring Victor Garber—a show which, according to *Variety*, was full of failings, including "Inept execution, a mediocre script, and a lack of action and suspense." The experience quickly convinced her that she'd be better off sticking to music.

But by 1986, the frustration was really setting in. She kept coming close to record deals, only to have them fade again. So when Bill Leopold announced that Chris Blackwell, the head of Island Records, was coming to see her, it was hard for Melissa to become too worked up. She'd been here before and nothing had happened. Yes, it was exactly what she wanted, but the chance of anything happening seemed more and more remote.

Blackwell had founded Island Records some twenty years before, initially to release Jamaican music in England. Since then the label had taken off in larger and more varied directions, helping to make international superstars out of a number of artists, including Bob Marley and U2. He still took a very hands-on approach with the music, going out and listening to new acts himself, and was willing to sign them on the spot if he was impressed enough.

When he arrived at the Que Sera Sera, Melissa knew nothing about him.

"I did not know who he was," she told *Musician*. "He just seemed like this really serious, beach-dressing English guy. He came in when I was singing. I sang three originals and a Joan Armatrading song. He said, 'I like what you do. I like your soul.' Well, he didn't actually say it that well."

Like many others before him, Blackwell was taken with what he heard, and saw the potential in Melissa's music.

"I was impressed by the passion she had for her performance," he said. "I thought at the time that potentially the next big rock 'n' roll star like Bruce Springsteen would be a girl. I thought, and still think, that she's the most likely to fill that role." He was astonished she didn't already have a recording contract, and told her so.

"I was amazed . . . that somebody of this obvious sort of strength had not been signed by anybody. I spoke to her after the show and said, 'I'd like to sign you to the label.' "

Those were the kinds of words guaranteed to rekindle the excitement in a singer's heart. Especially when, unlike the others, Blackwell's interest didn't vanish. He told Melissa that he wanted her on his label, and by the time the weekend arrived, she was an Island Records artist.

"I refuse to buy the idea that it's harder for women to make it in rock than men," she speculated later. "It's all how you handle yourself. I was signed because of my ability as a musician, not because of, or in spite of, my gender."

It was an interesting point of view, and perhaps typical that she chose to define herself, not by gender, but as a musician, a definition she's chosen to keep. But it made the situation a little too cut and dried. The fact that she *was* a woman had to be taken into account. In rock, women had never been taken quite as seriously as men; it remained a very masculine medium, giving women the choice of trying to outdo the men (as Lita Ford did for a while) or becoming overtly feminine and sultry. Melissa stayed away from both extremes, steering more of a middle course.

After the years of waiting, her big moment happened quickly. No months of build-up and negotiation, dealing with A & R men and lawyers, contracts going back and forth. She'd dealt with the top man, and it had been simple.

Maybe it had been too simple. She now had the opportunity to make an album of her songs, but other than that, nothing had really changed. Her contract didn't bring her a lot of money. Melissa Etheridge wasn't going to become an overnight star after putting her name on a piece of paper. She still had to perform at Que Sera Sera five nights a week in order to pay her rent and buy groceries. Even so, her life had taken an important turn.

The details of her contract were never revealed, but it was probably initially for one record, with an option on a second. The advance paid would have been relatively small—Melissa was an unknown quantity, and though Blackwell liked her material, he was still taking a risk in the marketplace.

Bill Leopold, who'd spent the last three years believing in her, and doing everything in his power to bring her to the attention of the major labels, knew how much of a breakthrough the recording contract was. Island had a good reputation for working with its artists and developing them. If Melissa could make a good, solid first album, from there things would move of their own accord. He knew, maybe even more than she did, that one day she'd be a star.

None of that could begin to happen, though, until she'd made that first record. She had plenty of work to do. Musicians had to be selected, Melissa had to go through her songs and decide which would work best. Then there were the matters of which studio and producer to use.

Before she began work on the album, she had another break. Now she was a legitimate recording artist, Melissa was asked to submit songs for the soundtrack of *Weeds,* an upcoming major movie starring Nick Nolte. So before she could even get her feet wet with her own record, she was hurriedly recording pieces for another project, one of which—"I Wanna Go Home"—would make the final cut.

Initially, Blackwell had wanted to produce Melissa's album himself. A man with a good ear, he'd done this for other artists on his label, and it would have been a wonderful sign of company acceptance. Business commitments prevented it, however, so he suggested Jim Gaines, a music business veteran who'd been behind the board for records by Journey, Huey Lewis and the News, and Eddie Money. All those acts had sold plenty of albums and made the charts more than once in their day, although their day seemed to have passed.

Still, when the boss suggested someone, you didn't turn around and say no. At least not if you were a new artist who'd been waiting for this break for a long time.

So, toward the end of 1986, Melissa and her new band, bassist Kevin McCormick and drummer Craig Krampf, went into the studio. The sessions were spread over a few months, with plenty of intense work. Melissa had hoped for something that would capture the way she came across live—raw, vital, and with the other instruments, even more powerful than her solo show—true rock 'n' roll. Gaines, however, seemed to have other ideas. He had a vision of a very full sound, not unlike the other artists he'd produced. Since he was calling the shots, and since she didn't know the band well yet, Melissa gave way.

By the time they'd finished ten tracks, what was on tape sounded nothing like the woman Blackwell had loved in the bar. Melissa was still there, but she was playing over layers and layers of pop music. It might have been good, but it wasn't the kind of record Blackwell wanted from Melissa Etheridge.

"Blackwell hated them. I thought, 'That's it, my career's over.' "

And it might well have been. Blackwell had given Melissa her shot, and she'd blown it. But it hadn't been her fault. She'd dutifully listened to the producer she'd been paired with and taken his word as gospel.

Having passed this hurdle, she wasn't about to give up. Blackwell hadn't liked what he'd heard, but she knew she could sound much better, more like herself. So did her new band. After working together in the studio for a few months they'd become friends. McCormick said to her, "Look, we can make this album together. Your songs are straightforward. They're easy to record. All we need is four days."

Melissa and Leopold went back to Blackwell and made the pitch. By now 1987 was more than half over. The obvious fear was that Blackwell had completely lost interest and moved on to other things. But he had believed in her enough to sign her. He understood Melissa's potential, and in the end decided to give her another chance. She'd have the four days in the studio that she required.

By then she'd acquired another friend, Niko Bolas, a recording engineer and producer, who was happy to work with her. They booked the studio time. Melissa, McCormick, and Krampf spent a time rehearsing the ten songs they'd be covering. Bolas wanted to go even further with the idea of a lean approach. Since Melissa was such a dynamic live performer, why not record all the tracks live? There'd be the rough, spontaneous feel. Any overdubs could be added later.

Live recording was, of course, always risky. A single small mistake could ruin an entire take. With only four days to put ten songs on tape, that meant a great deal of perfection. Still, it was possible. If Melissa was going to put everything on the line, why not go the whole way?

On October 19, 1987, Bolas and the band trooped into Cherokee Studio in West Hollywood. It wasn't the fanciest place in town, but ample for their needs and budget.

The key for the sessions was preparation. That meant getting everything exactly right before commiting any music to tape. Once the drum kit was set up, there was the tedious process of going through and getting the sound of each drum perfect, positioning and repositioning microphones until Bolas and the rest of the band were satisfied. After that was complete, it needed to be repeated with the bass and Melissa's acoustic guitar, and finally her vocal microphone.

The process was laborious, but necessary. Some studio wizardry could be applied when it was all finished, but the emphasis here would be on raw and powerful.

The studio time involved long periods of boredom punctuated by brief periods of excitement when Melissa and the guys performed. Everyone knew this was make-it-or-break-it time.

Melissa had never been one to hold back in her singing, and now she gave her all on every take. She repeated songs again and again, hoping for the one magic time when it would all catch fire and go from the great to the remarkable.

Most of the songs had been in Melissa's repertoire for some time. Some had been cut for the aborted album. But four were brand new: "Chrome Plated Heart," "The Late September Dogs," "Watching You," and "Occasionally." On the last, the additional percussive sound came from Melissa banging the back of her guitar.

By October 23, the band was exhausted. The four days had been an intense experience, but a worthwhile one. Bolas had pulled, teased, and cajoled some outstanding performances from them, the flesh and bones of the record. All it needed now was a little texture, and that was set to happen over three days in November.

Bolas knew plenty of players in the music business, and he called on a few to add their talents to Melissa's songs. There were Waddy Wachtel, who'd made an enviable name as a session guitarist over the years; keyboardist Wally Badarou, who'd done plenty of work with others as well as putting out his own albums; Scott Thurston, another keyboard player (and former member of the Stooges, with Iggy Pop); as well as Johnny Lee Schell, for more guitar work. When their work was complete, all that remained was for Krampf to dub in some percussion to fill out the rhythm sound, and everything was done.

Not *quite* done. The tracks were all there, but they still had to be mixed, the levels set on the tracks to give something close to the final product. Bolas started the process almost as soon as the overdubs were completed, going to into A&M's Studio B with assistant engineer Bob Vogt on November 20, 1987, and working odd days until the beginning of December. In the middle of January he spent two days at the Complex with engineer Duane Seykora putting on the finishing touches. By January 19, 1988, Melissa had her record.

The work had been done remarkably cheaply and quickly. It wasn't uncommon for bands to spend six months just on the recording stage. In a good studio the costs could rapidly run into hundreds of thousands of dollars. Including overdubs and mixing, this album had been completed in fourteen days.

The big question was whether Chris Blackwell would like it. This was Melissa's last chance. If this version didn't work, it was unlikely he'd be willing to pay for any more studio time. All she knew was that she'd done her best, and felt proud of the results. Every song and performance was as good as it could be.

It was a huge relief when Blackwell finally heard the album—and loved it. *This* was the person he'd heard at Que Sera Sera, captured with all the rawness and vibrancy that made her stand out. *Melissa Etheridge,* as the record would be known ("Nice title, eh?" she would quip later), immediately went on the Island Records release schedule, to be issued in late May, a quick turnaround.

Now, finally, Melissa could begin to believe that it was all happening.

*F*OUR

*M*elissa couldn't have had a better present for her twenty-seventh birthday than seeing her first album in the stores. Seventeen years after she'd gone into her parents' basement and written her first song, she could hold the fruits of all her work. The sleeve summed it all up. Under the name was a picture of Melissa, head thrown back, eyes closed, fists clenched in front of her in what could have been either passion or victory, or both.

She wore a motorcycle jacket, a white T-shirt and jeans, wrists covered in bracelets, a look that spoke of toughness without being too threatening. It was rock 'n' roll, that was for sure, but somehow cleaner than punk.

What was immediately evident on playing the disc was that Melissa and her collaborators had put a great deal of thought into the arrangements. Much of the material was just the basic trio, very lean, no overdubs, but done without ever sounding too sparse. And where other musicians had added their parts, it had been to build tension in the songs, or hit a climax with a solo, rather than to flesh out any skeleton; the basic band had managed that perfectly well already.

With rock being something of a self-referential medium, it was almost inevitable that some of the material should suggest things that had gone before. The opening of "Similar Features," for example, recalled the Zombies' sixties hit, "Time of the Season" in its beat. Both "Don't You Need" and "Watching You" offered faint echoes of the Eagles' "Hotel California" in the way Melissa's guitar had been recorded, while the drums on "Don't You Need" touched back a couple of years to Don Henley's "Boys of Summer."

But those things did not detract from the album's impact. Instead, by offering a few familiar touches they actually made it easier for the listener to accept this new artist.

Melissa was front and center all the way through. Her acoustic guitar was prominent in the mix, as it needed to be, whether strumming or picking, to support that voice. And the voice came across as a remarkable instrument. It could beg, plead, accuse, confront, speculate. The slight sandpaper raspiness might have hinted at both Rod Stewart and Janis Joplin, but what jumped out of the mix was pure Melissa. The passion simply throbbed through every song. She had the ability to reach a level of intensity quickly in a song, then sustain it, and pull the listener in with her. When she said she was burning up in "Bring Me Some Water," you believed her. Here was someone who not only felt things, but felt them incredibly strongly.

The band played to those extremes of emotion. The arrangements were dramatic. Melissa would be accompanying herself, then the bass and drums would crash in to help punch home the chorus, or shift the dynamics from soft to loud to help make a lyrical point.

Even at its simplest, this was undoubtedly a rock album. "Occasionally" had nothing more than Melissa singing a capella, hitting the back of her guitar for rhythmic accompaniment. A capella is a difficult style in rock: many singers tend to waver on their pitch doing it, or, by stripping a song to the bare bones, reveal how weak the song really is. Neither happened here. Melissa's voice was as assured, as in control on this song as on the rest of the album. Even without the melodies of other instruments she could sound committed, intense, and musical.

But then again, she'd worked toward this record for a long time. Lyrically, all ten songs dealt with relationships. But they were hardly romantic in content. There was desire, a lot of jealousy, some regret—all the signs of romance on the rocks, words for dysfunctional lovers.

"I didn't realize it was so much about the same feelings. I just tried to put together my best, most passionate songs, and it turned out that my conflicts with jealousy and pain are the most powerful emotions. I haven't really had my heart smashed and stomped on. But I do have conflicts."

All were addressed to that genderless "You," a style Melissa had employed for a long time.

"It's the way I've always written," she explained in the *Chicago Sun-Times*, "but it's not a conscious effort on my part. I didn't realize I was doing a genderless thing, but then I saw how it made my music accessible to almost everyone. . . . When I look at my audience, I . . . see that everyone has problems in love, everyone has pain they need to share. You don't have to slap a 'male' or 'female' label on that."

It worked; the listener could read what he or she wanted into it. But there was no doubt that the white heat of passion was there for all forty-five minutes and fifty-two seconds of *Melissa Etheridge*. It was a nonstop roller coaster ride.

Keeping the instrumentation basic had been a big risk, certainly in an era when the synthesizer and the drum machine seemed to clutter up every tune on the radio. But it paid off handsomely. Melissa had been used to performing alone, and writing to just the strength and sound of her guitar and voice. She'd been playing many of the songs from the record that way for some time. If she could make them rock just doing that, then she didn't need much to make them more effective as rock songs. Indeed, as the aborted work with Jim Gaines had shown, convoluted arrangements only detracted from both her songs and her voice. Stripped down, everything came through: the words could sting, the guitar could ring, and the bass and drums provide an underlying rhythm, a backdrop that added color.

Artistically, the quality of the songs, the organic sound, and Melissa's voice and presence were more than enough to make the album stand out from the general mill of releases. But to be successful, it had to appeal to the public. It had to sell. That required good reviews, radio play, and plenty of exposure.

It may have helped Melissa's cause that so many music writers were calling 1988 "The Year of the Woman." Debut albums by Tracy Chapman and Toni Childs appeared that year. Sinead O'Connor had made a name for herself a year before with her first record. Edie Brickell, with her band the New Bohemians, had a big hit with "What I Am," and was touted as a new face. The press ran plenty of articles about them all, and the sudden surge of women playing music wasn't so much new as suddenly newsworthy.

To a point, *Melissa Etheridge* was lost in the shuffle. With its more traditional musical values, closer to what was generally termed "classic rock," it was classified as "mainstream," while the others, each in her own way, were doing something different.

While music magazines rhapsodized over the other artists, the critics for general interest publications took a closer look at *Melissa Etheridge*. In *People*, Ralph Novak said that "Etheridge's throaty, aggressively emotional, born-to-compete voice sounds like Bonnie Tyler [a woman who achieved fleeting fame with a single, "Total Eclipse of the Heart"]. Her music has a rigorous vitality, and there's an edge to it." The *New York Daily News* found her "a sensuous, dramatic vocalist with a countryish tinge who sounds convincing and honest as well. She is reminiscent of Janis Joplin and Kim

Carnes [who was notable for the hit "Bette Davis Eyes"], except she has more control and focus." Those were all nice words, but they did little more than place Melissa in a continuum of raspy-throated women singers. Her individuality—even the fact that, unlike most of her predecessors, she wrote all her own material, and that she *rocked*—were ignored.

At least Canada's *Chatelaine* recognized her potential when the reviewer claimed that "she has every chance of being the star of the nineties entirely on her own," and calling her "one of the most bluntly sexual singers since Janis Joplin . . . her songs are some of the most unambiguously raunchy any woman has ever written." *Audio*, however, wondered if that wouldn't prove to be a dead end. While seeing that Melissa "possesses real charisma which shines through the pain," writer Michael Tearson felt that her greatest challenge would be "finding a wider subject for her songs."

Initially, the record didn't get much radio airplay. "Similar Features" had been released as a single a month before the album even appeared, only to vanish without a trace, and when "Don't You Need" came out in June 1988, its fate was similar. Then a few stations began to pick up on "Bring Me Some Water," and things began to snowball—in a small way. The album didn't rush to the top of the charts, but it did manage to lodge in the lower reaches of the Billboard Top 200. What Melissa needed to do was capitalize on that.

The way for her to do that was to tour, doing what she did so well—playing live for an audience. Over the spring and summer of 1988 she played some dates on the West Coast, opening for Lyle Lovett, and then the newly reformed Little Feat. Those were club dates, where she felt completely at home, close to the crowd. Her music might have had the big stadium sound, but within herself she wasn't ready for those venues yet.

A full tour was set for the fall, with Melissa opening for Bruce Hornsby before taking off on a few headlining dates of her own. Before that happened, though, she had a big event—a homecoming of sorts. She played at the Lone Star in Kansas City, Missouri, topping the bill and selling four hundred tickets, not bad for someone who remained largely unknown.

To go back home and do that was a triumph. Her parents could hear her, and see what their daughter was capable of. And she was able to play a real club there instead of the Lavaranda Lounge.

Life should have been good. Unfortunately, a few things in it weren't working as well as they might have. Melissa had been in a relationship for the past two years, and now, with the attention she was receiving, it was collapsing.

"The relationship . . . suffered from my sudden stardom," she said. "I had been physically there in the relationship for two years, and then suddenly I was gone, out on the road. But it wasn't the right relationship anyway."

What she had absolutely no way of knowing was that the start of what would be the right relationship was just around the corner.

To help push the album farther up the charts, Island agreed to finance a video for "Bring Me Some Water." It was gradually receiving more and more airplay, and a video in rotation on VH1 or MTV could make a major difference in album sales.

The shoot was set for September, on the second night of her first tour. Working as an assistant director was a woman named Julie Cypher. Without knowing anything about her, Melissa felt an immediate, "very physical" attraction. But Julie was heterosexual. She was even married, to the actor Lou Diamond Phillips, who'd become a film star the year before, taking the lead role of Richie Valens in *La Bamba*.

To Julie's astonishment and consternation, she found herself equally attracted to Melissa.

"I was drawn to her," she said. "But it never occurred to me that I could be a lesbian."

They talked, as much as time allowed. For now, though, there was nothing that they could do. Melissa had too much going on in her life, between her career and a relationship that was crumbling. Julie had suddenly been given plenty to think about. She'd always thought of herself as straight, all the time she'd been growing up in Texas. At twenty-three she thought she knew what she wanted: marriage, working toward directing her own films, kids someday. But even after a short while it wasn't working out the way she'd planned.

"The marriage was a troubled one," she explained. "Lou and I were really young, and Hollywood's a big place when you've just come from Texas. We thought, 'Well, we'll just get married and we'll have each other no matter what.' "

Like many others, their paths had started to diverge as careers beckoned. And now, from one brief meeting, Julie had to reexamine everything she believed she understood about herself, all the way to her fundamental assumptions.

All Julie and Melissa could do was keep in touch. There was definitely something between them, an electricity, a chemistry; they both knew that. As to whether they'd ever have a chance to explore it, only time would tell.

The Bruce Hornsby tour took Melissa to the East Coast and up into Canada before she left for a few dates on her own. Neither Providence, Rhode Island, nor Washington, D.C., brought in full houses, but when she took her act back west, things improved. In Boulder, Los Angeles, and San Francisco she was able to sell out clubs—a good feeling.

Then it was time to take her music over the borders. Both Canada and Australia had been especially receptive to Melissa's music; the record had gone platinum in both countries. And, of course, it was important to break the influential English market. That didn't happen. But a brief English tour did give Melissa the chance to hear herself on the radio for the first time.

"We were rushing to catch a train and all of a sudden 'Similar Features' came on. I said, 'I know that song.' Then it hit me. I sat there and cried."

At home, the "Bring Me Some Water" video received plenty of airplay on VH1, and the album continued to sell steadily, if not spectacularly, throughout 1988, managing to remain in the lower reaches of the Top 200. It was obvious that Melissa had the ability to move beyond cult status. All she needed was wider exposure. That opportunity occurred when "Bring Me Some Water" was nominated for a Grammy Award. The news both surprised and delighted her. Her album hadn't sold in huge quantities, but there was plenty of support within the industry for her work; she had people in her corner, trying to give her greater recognition.

She knew that winning was unlikely, given the lack of popular familiarity with her name. But the show offered something almost as valuable as the statuette: a chance to appear live, singing the song, in front of a television audience of some forty million people. She'd already recorded some of the material for her second record during a few days in January, but the "legs" on her debut were proving to be longer than anyone had anticipated.

The timing was perfect. Melissa and her band, which now included guitarist Bernie Larsen and new drummer Mauricio Fritz Lewak, as well as bassist Kevin McCormick, played a couple of warm-up dates in California, selling out two shows each in San Francisco and San Rafael. After the Grammy show, they planned to embark on their first long cross-country tour.

Melissa did not walk away with a Grammy award that night, but the statuette would simply have been the icing on the cake. Her performance was more than enough to make people sit up and notice a real new talent. Intense, raw, and passionate, she injected some rock 'n' roll into the glitzy showbiz event the Grammys had become. In a world of synthesized pop, she was real.

The performance had an immediate effect on her album. After forty-four weeks sitting near the bottom of the album charts, *Melissa Etheridge* began to climb, and by April would hit number 32, en route to a peak twelve places higher, and bring Melissa a gold record for sales of half a million copies. "Similar Features," reis-

Melissa stops for a photo at the 1990 Grammy Awards, where she served as a presenter.

(Above) Melissa performs in Los Angeles, 1992. (Below) In 1993, Melissa won her first Grammy (Best Rock Vocal Performance—Female), for "Ain't It Heavy."

Melissa and her partner, Julie Cypher, attend a movie premiere in 1993.

(Above) Melissa performs in concert in February 1994 at the State Theatre in New Brunswick, New Jersey. After the show (right), New Jersey native Jon Bon Jovi pays her a visit.

Melissa Etheridge, Phoebe Snow, and k.d. lang (left to right) were among the performers at "The Beat Goes On," an AIDS benefit held on June 24, 1994, at the Beacon Theatre in New York City.

Melissa recaptures the spirit of the sixties as a Woodstock 1994 performer.

Renowned drag performer Lady Bunny, Melissa, and Julie Cypher (left to right) share stories over drinks following a Tammy Wynette concert in October 1994.

In March 1995, Etheridge won her second Grammy, for "Come to My Window."

sued as a single, finally clicked with an audience and reached number 94 in the Hot 100. Her career was taking off.

Her live dates were selling out, and not just on the West Coast this time. Across the country—Phoenix, Tucson, St. Louis, Chicago, Columbus—audiences were beginning to fall under her spell. This was exactly what she needed, to be out there performing, letting people experience the enormous power she could generate live. With ticket sales staying brisk all over America, the tour was extended to keep Melissa and the band on the road until the middle of May. Following a short break, they played dates in western Canada, after which they took three more days in the studio to finish recording the next album.

That was the way of the music business. When you were hot, you had to take advantage of it. You stayed on the road, traveling for so many hours every day, using the charge of each show to keep you going. It wasn't easy. You really had to want success to put up with the endless discomfort, the lack of sleep, the constant problems of the road. For Melissa, things were still at the low-budget stage. She had no fancy air-conditioned buses with plenty of room to stretch out and relax between gigs, or an army of help to ensure everything was set up and maintained perfectly. This tour was far more rough and ready, with too many people crammed into a van, hour upon hour of boredom broken by the high of performance before a return to the drudgery. But, even done in this basic manner, touring was an expensive proposition. A day off was a day that brought in no money, so those were kept to an absolute minimum. There had to be *some* allowances, of course; Melissa's voice simply couldn't stand the strain of performing night after night after night. For the most part, though, she had to keep moving. With the record doing well, the single scraping into the charts, and a powerful feedback from the audience at every gig, the mood remained upbeat.

It all climaxed with a series of outdoor dates in July, opening again for Little Feat in the East and Midwest.

"It was almost a double billing and we got a good reaction," she said later.

Then, finally, Melissa and the boys could get home to Los Angeles, sleep, relax, and rub the road from their bones for a while. Melissa and Julie Cypher had remained in touch, talking on the phone, even seeing each other when Melissa was at home. After several months the feelings of mutual attraction hadn't vanished, but Julie was still with Lou Diamond Phillips. She had yet to tell him about Melissa and the way things seemed to be developing. It was hard. Both Julie and Melissa understood what they wanted from each other—to be together—but reaching that stage seemed almost impossible. The time never seemed right for Julie to tell Lou, even though the marriage already had problems.

On Melissa's side, just because she was home didn't mean she had much time to relax. Just off the road, she had all the details of a new album to deal with: the mixing, the packaging, handling the ever-increasing requests for interviews and photo sessions. Having worked so hard to get this far, she wasn't about to turn down opportunities for press. This was, after all, her career. And it was beginning to get crazy.

She was becoming familiar with exhaustion, and all the demands on her time. Sometimes that meant being willing to go to industry conventions, spending time with big record retailers and radio people, the ones who, down the line, could help her sell albums. It was something many artists were reluctant to do. Melissa was always willing, though, and always friendly to these people who were, in their own way, a part of the music business. Being nice and polite had been instilled in her from a young age; it came naturally, and helped her create a lot of goodwill in the business. She was on the way up, but there was no attitude about her, none of the star tripping or egomania that seemed so prevalent among singers and bands. Melissa knew what she wanted, and what she believed she could achieve. She really had a shot at making it to the top, or at least somewhere near to doing what no woman had done in over twenty years.

Of those women who'd released debut albums at the same time as hers, the Class of '88, a couple had burned very brightly, then faded. Tracy Chapman enjoyed critical acclaim, strong record sales, and a hit single with "Fast Car." But although critics quite fairly deemed her a tremendous talent, and her sophomore album also sold well, after that her presence in the music scene diminished until 1996. Toni Childs was briefly lauded by a few writers; her album, however, never managed to catch the attention of the buying public. Edie Brickell's "What I Am" had done well, but she remained a one-hit wonder, eventually marrying Paul Simon and issuing another record—which he produced—several years later.

Melissa was the only out-and-out rocker, the only one to challenge the boys on their own turf. She hadn't won yet, but she'd gained some ground. The touring had helped, but her appearance at the Grammys had made a huge difference. A lot of people knew who she was these days, and some of them had bought her album. For a first step it was a good, long stride. AOR (Album Oriented Rock) radio had taken to her. Her music fit in well alongside the classic groups—the Eagles, Bob Seger, even her hero Springsteen. It was good, solid, American rock. The fact that it wasn't cutting edge in any way stopped her from being seen as hip, but that was fine. Melissa didn't have any pretensions to hipness. All she wanted to be able to do was play her music her way for the people who wanted to listen. She was a rock 'n' roller, a midwestern girl with midwestern tastes and values, making the kind of music she'd loved since childhood.

Obviously she was doing something right. *Melissa Etheridge* had gone gold: at least half a million people had liked her sound enough to go out and spend money on it. But that alone didn't make her a star. The standards in the music business had changed over recent years, to the point where a gold record was seen as only moderately successful. Going platinum—selling more than a million copies—had become the new criterion, and that was something few new artists achieved, other than those who definitely appealed to a teen market.

What Melissa had achieved was a base that she could expand on, so that her second, or perhaps her third, album could break that magic number. She was already able to headline, and sell out, shows in clubs. The aim was for her to move to larger venues as her popularity grew, until she'd at last be in the big arenas that seemed ideal for her music.

As a debut, *Melissa Etheridge* had had much to recommend it. Good songs that injected new passion into a genre that needed it; strong performances, fairly basic and stripped down, but which, through intelligent arranging, managed to feel full rather than sparse. A tough, live sound. And above all, the voice. This was Melissa's real calling card, something that truly separated her from the pack. With its raw edge and sexual power, it could send emotional messages, and hit the listener in the gut as well as the brain. Rock, after all, hadn't begun as cerebral music.

It's a truism that artists spend all their lives preparing for their first record. After that they're supposed to turn around and bring out something new, something even better, within a year, which all too often leads to the phenomenon known as the sophomore slump. Many artists write new material too fast, or dredge up old songs that didn't quite make the cut the first time around. Would Melissa fall prey to it? August 1989 would bring the answer.

FIVE

On first hearing, the new album, named *Brave and Crazy,* didn't seem as immediately appealing as its predecessor. For a start, it was that most unusual of things, a rock album that contained no real guitar solos. Only one track, "Royal Station 4/16," came close, and even then Melissa's voice remained in front of the mix, wailing, while the guitar stayed well back, pulling off small, bluesy licks, dueling with the harmonica played by guest star Bono, the singer of U2.

Like *Melissa Etheridge,* this album was recorded quickly, mostly live, in six days, three in January 1989 (24, 25, 26), and three more in May (24, 25, 26), with Niko Bolas again producing, as Melissa and the band took short breaks from touring. Surprisingly, its sound was even less polished than the debut, very much up front, leaping out of the speakers.

In most bands, too often the rhythm guitar tends to remain in the background. In this case, it was easy to hear Melissa's twelve-string Ovation. Most of the time, in fact, its rhythm carried the song, working with the drums, while the bass punctuated with short breaks, and Bernie Larsen's electric guitar added occasional color.

That alone was unconventional enough to make the record stand out. The feeling it gave was lean and urgent—rough and ready on the surface, but with a great deal of consideration given to the arrangements underneath. Much of the material had been written on the road, during the tours in support of the first album. Melissa had found that the songs could pour out of her anywhere she happened to be.

"Well, I've written for so long that I've learned to store things up. I'm really lucky that way. . . . The world goes by and you just open up your mind and there it is. Or in a hotel, on a day off. Hours. You just call for food and you don't need to do anything but . . . be there."

Melissa clearly wasn't about to let herself be pigeonholed; *Brave and Crazy* definitely was not a clone of *Melissa Etheridge*. With the exception of "No Souvenirs" (which had been released as the album's first single, and failed to reach the charts), the record was moving in a different direction, one that was decidedly more individual. Love, and particularly the loss of it, was once again the predominant lyrical theme, but this time it was matched against rougher musical textures. The melodies and choruses were less obvious, less hummable. Overall, if the disc brought anything to mind, it was the early records of Bruce Springsteen, the albums Melissa had played over and over again when she was younger, and that had influenced her so much then; her vision was becoming grander and more cinematic.

There was also a very funky element to *Brave and Crazy* that hadn't been on the first album. It leaped out of the title track, with its scratchy twelve-string rhythm and powerful dynamics, moving from soft to loud and back again, with the bass as a virtual lead instrument, and "Testify," which Melissa had written with bassist Kevin McCormick, while "Royal Station 4/16" had a groove that wandered very close to blues.

Whether they really worked or not, those elements made the record a progression. As a songwriter, Melissa was beginning to explore what she could do with a band behind her, really using their talents to give shape to her songs. While the out-and-out rock of *Melissa Etheridge* had come out of her solo performances at Que Sera Sera and other places on the Long Beach scene, where the only power she had was herself, on her second album she was writing for a group and experimenting with the possibilities of that sound. Her voice, and her guitar, remained very much in the foreground, but the other instruments were completely integrated into the arrangements.

Brave and Crazy also showed that Melissa had gained real control over her voice, a benefit of the touring and the constant pressure to perform. She could still sound like she was giving every drop of emotion to a song, pouring it all out, without the wildness that had been evident in her singing on *Melissa Etheridge*. It wasn't restraint; instead, she'd learned how to use her voice more effectively.

The album did have its guest musicians, but they were used sparingly. Scott Thurston's keyboards filled out the sound of "No Souvenirs," and Waddy Wachtel provided the brief electric guitar runs on "Royal Station 4/16," trading those licks with Bono's harmonica (a strange choice, since Bono was known neither for playing harmonica nor playing blues, or even conventional rock—though he was part of a well-established band also signed to Island).

The acoustic side of Melissa's writing, which had produced songs like "The Late September Dogs" and "Occasionally" on her debut, was less in evidence here. The closest she came was the Springsteenish "You Can Sleep While I Drive," a tale of hitting the road, and even that was very much a band piece.

After all the mixing was finished and the master tapes were passed to Island for release, it was clear to the powers that be that, beyond "No Souvenirs," there was no obvious single on *Brave and Crazy*, nothing likely to generate a hit. This was a work to be taken as a whole, a complete document rather than a collection of individual tracks. Melissa had established a core audience that would go with her into this slightly darker musical territory. But would any others follow?

Whatever the people at the label might have thought privately, in public they were standing firm behind *Brave and Crazy*, ready to give it a big push. *Melissa Etheridge* had done well enough to warrant that. From the packaging alone, it was obvious that Island had spent more money on this project. The sleeve for *Melissa Etheridge* had been simple: one photograph and a reproduction of the lyrics. The booklet that accompanied the new record was packed with black-and-white pictures of Melissa, alone and with the band—definitely a deluxe presentation, and one whose light-and-dark contrasts also echoed the more shadowy nature of the musical contents.

New York didn't seem to think *Brave and Crazy* was any less of an album than her debut. Opening with the sentence "If you buy only one album between now and the end of the decade, make sure it's by Melissa Etheridge," its review was praise all the way. Without really discussing the music, the reviewer indulged in a brief analysis of the lyrics, praising "You Can Sleep While I Drive" as "a feminine version of Bruce Springsteen's 'Born to Run,' " finding kind words for "My Back Door" ("the album's best song") and "No Souvenirs" ("the catchiest song she's yet recorded"), before concluding that in an age of increasing technology "Her antidote is to get extremely honest and personal through her music."

In *Stereo Review*, Ron Givens noted that "Melissa Etheridge makes folk-rock, with the emphasis on the rock." Unfortunately, he found her to be a person of extremes, both in her singing and her writing, with "soft expectancy in the verses and hard pounding in the choruses." While he liked individual songs, saying they were "quite effective," he felt that an entire album of Melissa Etheridge was just too much: "the repetitiveness and narrowness of her music get a little tiresome."

Ralph Novak, writing in *People,* understood that "her music has a distinctive integrity, a style that affects the head and heart as well as the ear." He obviously liked this "exciting second album" since it "always keeps a strong melodic presence in her singing." Melissa, he thought, had a golden future: "She belongs among the major figures of the record business—her talents and tastes may well help define the music of her generation."

At this stage, such praise was, perhaps, a slight exaggeration. Nonetheless, *Brave and Crazy* showed just how far Melissa had come, and how fast. On its release it entered the Billboard album charts at 69, rising in three weeks to 27, an impressive display that boded well for the album's sales.

Instead of organizing a large tour to launch the record this time, the label adopted a slightly different strategy. Melissa was booked into clubs in four cities where she'd done well (Music Hall Theatre in Toronto, Canada; Park West in Chicago; the Bottom Line in New York; and the Roxy Theater in Los Angeles), playing five consecutive nights in each.

Every single show was a sellout. Indeed, tickets for all the concerts at the Roxy, with a capacity of 425 people, were snapped up in twenty minutes.

"I had to tell some of my friends I couldn't get them tickets," Melissa said.

Of course, those wouldn't be the only live shows she'd play for *Brave and Crazy.* Having finished the album, she was eager to be performing for crowds again. She had mapped out virtually a year on the road. Following the sellout shows, she and the band were off to Europe for thirty-two dates, before returning to play shows in America, then jetting off at Island's instigation, for a tour of the Far East—Australia, New Zealand, and Japan. She was popular there, and it offered the band a chance to hone the material. Only then would the *real* U.S. tour begin, stretching all the way through November 1990.

It was a daunting schedule, but Melissa was more than ready for it. Playing music was her life—not just recording, but playing for people. That was how she'd begun, and it was still something that gave her a thrill.

Likewise, audiences loved her. *Variety* reviewed one of her five shows at the Bottom Line, commenting that "the faithful were screaming themselves hoarse. . . . If she can get her earthy rockers played on radio outside of AOR, she'll be a natural for theaters or as an arena band's opening act."

One true indication that Melissa already was making musical waves was her appearance in ads for Kaman Adamas guitars, which made the Ovation guitars she used. But this was an age of endorsements and sponsorships. Bands sought corporate help from beer to perfume companies to cover the enormous, constantly escalating costs of touring. While Melissa wasn't seeking that—by her own admission, she wasn't a fan of sponsorship—she was willing to endorse products she truly believed in, and she'd become a big enough name for a company to approach her.

"I've loved Ovation guitars since I was fourteen," she explained. "I've always liked them. . . . Last year, they made a guitar for me and they're trying to design a string for me that won't break, because I break a lot of strings. . . . I don't mind telling other musicians about what I like to use, play, and believe in. They don't give me anything, but they do give me good deals."

Although none of the singles from *Brave and Crazy* reached the charts, the album received wider radio play, pushing it up to 22 on the Billboard Top 200, and keeping it just below the Top 20 for some time, bringing Melissa her second gold record. The tour helped keep sales moving, but it would be another year before the record (as well as *Melissa Etheridge*) finally broke the platinum barrier.

After the overseas dates, Melissa and her band were more than ready to go out and conquer America. In many parts of the country she'd now reached the level of selling out small theaters, where the audience would number two thousand or more, a distinct leap up the popularity ladder. In Minneapolis, Jon Bream of the *Minneapolis Star and Tribune* found her "a remarkable, emotionally charged singer of the caliber of Bruce Springsteen and Janis Joplin. She had the near-capacity crowd of twenty-five hundred hanging on her every word and saluting her like a pop icon."

Melissa's willingness to spend a long, long time on the road, honing her skills and working the fans in the small clubs, was winning them over. When she played the Beacon Theater in New York, selling out another four shows, *Variety* found much the same reaction as in Minneapolis.

"Melissa Etheridge effortlessly fills the stage with her punchy rock and just-a-girl-with-a-guitar persona. Ecstatic audience response suggests that, even without hit singles, Etheridge is well on her way to becoming a major star."

In fact, critics faulted her only for performing no new material, and for her cover of Marvin Gaye's "Let's Get It On," a song she'd been performing for some time. In truth, the song was not especially suited to her style. Her music didn't have the teasing silkiness that had been so much a part of Gaye's performance. But Melissa's shows certainly had a sexual element.

"I like to bring that sexual energy out by seducing the audience, and, when it's there, building on it. I would like to say that, maybe, going to a concert of mine is like foreplay."

What stood beyond question was the fact that Melissa was moving up in the music scene, selling out venues all across the country. She hadn't quite reached the arenas yet, but now that seemed to be simply a matter of time.

Melissa's private life had moved onto a stronger footing, too. After knowing each other for eighteen months, and wondering what would happen, she and Julie had gotten together, in January of 1990—right in the middle of Melissa's tours to promote the album.

Julie had finally come to accept her feelings for Melissa and knew they weren't going to go away. It was love, on both sides. After taking time to sort out her own feelings, she explained the situation to her husband, Lou Diamond Phillips.

"It certainly wasn't something he expected," she told *The Advocate*, "but I don't think it threw him for too much of a loop because he's a very open and loving person. When he met Melissa he realized what a wonderful person she is, he could see how the two of us clicked so well."

Their marriage had been in trouble for some time. Julie needed, and wanted, Melissa, and Melissa wanted her. Julie and Lou finally separated—although their divorce wouldn't become official until 1992—and Julie moved into the house Melissa had purchased in the Hollywood Hills.

After waiting, anticipating, and wondering for so long, they were together. But it was just for a short time. Melissa was due back on the road, leaving Julie alone to settle into her new home.

Melissa had known about her own sexuality for ten years. She'd had the time to become comfortable with it. For Julie, though, this was a new world, and one of the challenges she had to face was coming out to her family.

"When I called them and said, 'I'm in love with a woman,' they were, like, 'Ooooh, uh, okay.' "

Initially, her mother was surprised.

"She had been married, after all," Betty Cypher said. "But I met Melissa and liked her, and that made it more understandable."

And to Julie's father, Dick, it was simply "not that big a deal now."

To a loving, supportive family, Julie's new relationship seemed fine. But there were still so many new things, new ideas, that Julie had to come to terms with.

From the beginning, almost from the time they met, Melissa was convinced that Julie was the right person for her. When she moved in, it seemed to cement the connection between them.

"I wasn't so worried about her straightness," Melissa said. "She's the perfect example of people being attracted to each other's souls—whether male or female. So I wasn't worried that I was just an 'experiment.' Of course, there were some different lifestyle things she had to adjust to"—in particular being surrounded by lesbians and musicians.

However, given that Julie had been married to a movie star and was used to the bright lights of a public life, the adjustment was easier than it might otherwise have been. Julie was a girl from Texas, that was true, but she'd spent several years in Hollywood by now. She knew actors and directors. She had plans to direct her own movies. She didn't know musicians, but she was going to have the chance to learn very quickly.

"Believe me," she laughed later, "it's harder to be in love with a musician than with a lesbian—that's the real bottom line."

Until Melissa finished her time on the road, with a final concert in Evanston, Illinois, on November 18, the couple had very little time to spend together. Even when Melissa had breaks in June and July, she was exhausted. Each time, just as they were getting used to being together, Melissa had to leave again.

On the surface, the couple seemed like a pairing of opposites. Julie was a vegetarian, and active with the organization PETA. Melissa, with her strong midwestern background, still ate meat. Julie was neat; Melissa, by her own admission, was a slob. Melissa lived in T-shirts, jeans, and flannel shirts—comfortable clothes. Julie, on the other hand, was fastidious about her grooming, even down to her makeup and lipstick, which, Melissa admitted, "I hate wearing . . . every day."

Somehow, those opposites managed to complement each other. Julie was perfectly content to live with Melissa's menagerie of cats and dogs, even with the shark that inhabited the pool outside.

The only thing that could have made it better was if Melissa could have been completely open about their relationship. Friends and family knew, but as far as her fans were concerned, it had to remain unmentioned. She was gaining ground, on the path to real stardom, and in George Bush's Republican America, where "family values" had become a prime issue, it was debatable how a public coming-out statement would have been received.

Of course, some of her audience, particularly the women, suspected the truth. For the most part, though, the people who bought her albums and attended her concerts never gave it much thought. They simply assumed that Melissa was part of the heterosexual majority. With her career at a delicate stage—she was doing well, but with only two albums she wasn't yet fully established in the public consciousness—and with her appeal to a very mainstream rock audience, why say anything right now?

"I was out professionally," she explained. "Everyone I knew, everyone I worked with, everyone in my record company knew I was a lesbian."

Did it really need to go beyond that? Was it important or even necessary for the crowds to know about her private life? The answer was no. However, that didn't stop reporters from asking. In an age of celebrity, people wanted to know everything about their idols. But this was something that wouldn't be published until Melissa was ready. She'd been willing to talk about it with a few select journalists, but always strictly off the record, and with a promise of absolute privacy that the journalists respected.

She already had a large lesbian following, which dated from her days playing the Long Beach bars, and which had grown as she became a national figure. But such a following might have been understandable simply because of her stature as a female performer. Of those women whose debut albums appeared in 1988, Melissa was the only one who'd been able to stay the course and even manage to increase her popularity. Toni Childs and Edie Brickell had both vanished.

All that left Melissa as something of a figurehead, a role model, and an inspiration to women, be they straight or lesbian. She'd gone out and done it. She'd proved that women could rock, that they could attract audiences and sell records without cramming themselves into spandex, having big hair, or showing acres of cleavage.

She had always been herself, totally honest, and she'd succeeded on her voice, her songs, and her shows.

The fact that none of her songs was addressed to a "him" (although "Testify," from *Brave and Crazy*, arguably could be heard that way) meant that the lesbian segment of her audience was very much included. They had no need to change the pronouns to feel a part of the song. Her inclusiveness, as she'd said, was quite deliberate.

Like Springsteen or John Mellencamp, much of the audience who bought her records and attended her concerts came from the working class. The images she used—of driving, getting away from a small town, calls from pay phones, even the automobile analogy of "Chrome Plated Heart"—spoke innately and naturally of that background. Her parents might have been more middle-class, but Melissa knew exactly what she was talking about. In her lyrics she wasn't an observer, but a participant in that life. She understood how the passion could build in a heart like steam in a pressure cooker, how the small midwestern towns could frustrate and stultify, what it was like waiting for the release of a Friday night. She'd been there. It was her. She captured a spirit. Which was why, when she played, there was inevitably a strange mix of people in the crowds—the dudes whose lives revolved around souped-up cars, all long hair and muscles; the mall girls with their teased hair; baby boomers who'd found someone to compare with their magical Janis; and lesbians of all kinds. For one night, at least, they could come together in tolerance, to enjoy the music. For a performer to be able to make that happen was quite an achievement.

Still, it wasn't enough to make Melissa come out, however much she might have wanted to. America didn't seem ready to embrace an openly lesbian (or gay) rock star. Homosexuality stood at odds with the rock 'n' roll image many people held in their own minds. Never mind that statistically, one in ten people in the population was gay; the silent majority always managed to speak without saying a word.

"Plenty of my fans know," Melissa told reporter Barry Walters off the record in 1992. But even she knew that wasn't really enough. "I hate pussyfooting around the truth. That's not the kind of person I am."

And that especially was the case now that she'd found real love. The year of touring finished, she was able to settle in with Julie, to establish a life and relax.

The cycle of supporting *Brave and Crazy* was over; the record had run its course. For a year and a half it had been part of her life every single day, as she played songs from it, talked about it, relived it. Now that was done.

Because most of the material for that record had been written on the road, while she was out promoting *Melissa Etheridge* and establishing herself, there was a toughness, a feistiness to the songs. It wasn't the fake rock-chick kind that passed for strength in some heavy metal circles, but a sincere message about survival in a harsh world.

Whether the public would recognize the talent in her songs had hardly been a foregone conclusion. Many artists with great talent never manage to break through, spending years, even whole careers, in obscurity. Luck had played its part. Melissa had come along at exactly the right time to gain visibility, she had a voice that reminded listeners of one of rock's icons without being derivative, and VH1 had played her videos, making her name, and her sound, familiar to even greater numbers.

But for all those gains, there was still a long way to go. To all commercial purposes, two records that had only gone gold (although both would eventually go platinum) meant that she was still something of a cult artist, albeit one with a high profile who could— and should—break out into the real mainstream.

The question was, could she do that without compromising her music? She had yet to achieve a real hit single, one that cracked the Top 40. Neither of her albums had broken the barrier of the Top 20. Could it be that she was destined for a prominent place in rock's second division, one of the ones who could have been contenders but never quite managed the top rank? The answer, of course, had to be no.

She'd reached a plateau. Now she needed to climb from that. Part of it, perhaps, was that she needed to change her approach to recording. She'd taken her stripped-down, live-in-the-studio aesthetic about as far as it could go. Over the course of two albums it had worked well, even if on the first it had been a necessity instead of a deliberate tactic. What Melissa really needed now was a change of approach—something a bit fuller that might bring in more people who'd been put off by the rawness of her overall sound.

First, however, she needed a break. After three years of almost continuous work, she'd earned one. She wanted a chance to spend time with Julie, to recharge her creative batteries and write some new material.

That break would turn into something longer than she, or anyone else, had planned. Many people expected—and wanted—her to release another album in 1991. After all, *Brave and Crazy* had appeared in 1989. But it would be April 1992 before Melissa had anything new in the stores.

Even as she unwound and worked with the guitar or piano on new songs, the musical world around her was changing. What had so recently been called alternative music had exploded into the American consciousness. The sound had been there for a long time, but suddenly it had truly caught the attention of young record buyers. And so Nirvana's *Nevermind* and Pearl Jam's *10* rocketed up the album charts. "Smells Like Teen Spirit" became an unlikely hit single, an anthem for a whole new, disaffected generation. In the eyes of some journalists, Seattle became the center of the musical universe. The floodgates had broken, and new music poured through.

Much of it had a harder feel than the music that had gone before. While Pearl Jam was, at heart, just a hard rock band, it had an edge. Its lyrics, like Nirvana's *spoke* to a new generation that wasn't addressed by commercially successful music of previous years. It was as if, after fifteen years, America had finally turned, understood, and embraced punk.

Part of this revolution was the rise of bands that included women, or were all-female. They rocked; it never occurred to them that they couldn't. Kim Gordon played bass and sang in Sonic Youth (a group that had been around, mostly on the avant-garde side, for a number of years), and became a new sort of figurehead. In Seattle, the all-female band 7 Year Bitch emerged from the basement and found that their third show was opening for the Red Hot Chili Peppers in front of six thousand people. The times were most definitely a-changin'.

What did that mean for Melissa? She loved some of the new music.

"When I saw the video for 'Smells Like Teen Spirit,' I thought that was the coolest sound I ever heard. I used to keep MTV on all day long."

But there was no way she could play anything like that. It simply wasn't her. The overall effect it had was to push her music to the center. She'd been more or less in left field—not too far out, but definitely different, because she was a woman who could rock. Now the new left had arrived, and these alternative bands made Melissa completely mainstream.

"I think it's fabulous. When you have extremes, then the middle changes. Then I become the middle. When these girls are saying, 'Only women in our front row' and 'We're lesbian feminists, and we're all *aargh,*' and they're really crazy and scary, then I look really normal. They sort of balance out this far right."

As she knew, she'd never been a darling of MTV, which aimed directly at the youth market.

"I was never an MTV artist. I was never of the moment. I didn't wear the right clothes."

Now, even more than before, her music was taken up by VH1. She represented a sort of hipness that wasn't trendy. While she didn't consider herself to be a classic rock artist, much of her audience was among the people who would rather listen to Led Zeppelin than Soundgarden, Jimi Hendrix rather than Pearl Jam. Alternative would bypass many of them altogether.

That was fine. She'd found her niche quite easily. Now she needed to use that as a base, and expand on it. She'd achieved some success, but she hadn't yet won any laurels she could rest on. There were so many more things still to be achieved, personally and professionally.

And so, during the first half of 1991, surrounded by new domestic bliss, she worked on songs for the record that might make her a household name.

Sadly, everything was interrupted by tragedy. Her father, the man who'd ferried her to all those early gigs, who'd supported her when she came out to him, died of liver cancer. As he grew weaker, Melissa returned to Leavenworth to help take care of him.

"I was very close to him," she recalled, "and I actually saw him die. It's an amazing experience. Suddenly I was parenting him."

She had her theories about what had brought on his illness.

"He kept his anger about his alcoholic parents inside himself. His anger turned to cancer. The body can only hold that stress in for so long before it becomes something else."

She stayed and buried him and wept. He was gone, but his spirit would remain with her. When she would win her Grammy, she would dedicate the award to Julie and to the memory of her father, who had done so much to give her a start in music.

*S*ɪx

*F*rom the time recording began, it was apparent that *Never Enough* was going to be an experiment, completely different from Melissa's first two records. Like *Brave and Crazy* it was recorded at A&M Studios in Hollywood, but the similarities ended there. Niko Bolas, who had done such excellent work behind the console on the first two albums, wasn't involved in this one. Melissa took over the production herself, along with bassist Kevin McCormick, who returned with drummer Mauricio Fritz Lewak. The guests brought in on almost every track indicated that this album would have a much fuller, more complex and arranged sound, with plenty of keyboards included in the mix for a change, and even a cello part played with surprising ability by the actor Dermot Mulroney. "The Letting Go" brought Melissa's recording debut on the piano, while two other tunes had her playing electric guitar, something she did occasionally in concert, but hadn't yet done in the studio.

These were all thoughtful changes. While Melissa's first two albums had the fire of spontaneity from their quick recording, this was much more layered—the result of a longer, and more complex procedure. But then again, this was the first time she'd gone into the studio with songs she hadn't played live beforehand. It was, for all intents and purposes, Melissa's first real studio album. It was also, in its way, far more personal than its predecessors. Dedicated to her father, it seemed as if several of the songs referred to him, some quite overtly, like "Dance Without Sleeping"; others somewhat more obliquely, such as "The Letting Go," ostensibly about a lover giving up her hold on a relationship, but operating on a number of levels.

Never Enough arrived in the stores on March 17, 1992, almost two and a half years after *Brave and Crazy.* It had been ready by the fall of 1991, but the release was put back, not because of any problems Island Records had with her new musical feel, but simply because the fourth quarter of the year already had a number of "big" albums scheduled, notably U2's *Achtung Baby,* and they wanted to concentrate their energies on those. It was better, they rationalized, to wait, so they could work Melissa's record in the right way; otherwise, it could end up lost in the shuffle.

For Melissa, of course, that just meant added frustration. After months of work, putting her heart and soul into the music, winding herself up tight in anticipation of release, it just meant more anxiety, more waiting.

"For the past couple of months I've been in limbo," she said as March 17 approached. "Now I'm so eager."

The label had high expectations for *Never Enough;* that was certain. She had a core audience, and over the course of her career so far she'd carved out a strong position for herself in music. Even with "alternative" encroaching on the sales of mainstream figures, there was definitely a place for her—and that, everyone hoped, was on top of the charts.

"She's definitely the market leader in female rock figures right now," said Chris Blackwell, the man who'd originally believed in her music enough to sign her, "and she will consolidate that position after this record comes out."

The album's cover was definitely set to make an impact. It showed a shirtless Melissa, her back to the camera, holding an electric guitar by the neck. While her face wasn't visible, it was a powerful image, suggestive and sensual, and one which, in its own way, held faint echoes of one of her heroes: Bruce Springsteen on his *Born in the U.S.A.* record.

The picture, however, came about purely by accident, or good fortune, depending on your viewpoint. Melissa wanted something eye-catching.

"We live in a world of the vanishing album," she explained to the *Miami New Times*. "Before, you could do complicated things in the artwork of vinyl albums. Now the configurations are tiny. I wanted a CD cover people could see all the way across the record store and notice. Also, I have a big problem with fashion. I'd prefer not to have to wear anything."

She elaborated a little further in another interview.

"Sometimes I find myself thinking, 'What am I going to wear?' and that what I wear is such a statement. Well, I'm not labeled by what I wear, so I decided to not wear anything on the album cover."

During the photo shoot, once she'd had the inspiration to go topless, everyone except the photographer was asked to leave the studio. Melissa slipped off her shirt, picked up a guitar, and turned her back on the camera.

Amazingly, as relatively innocuous as the picture was, some people in the industry were surprised by the cover and its sexuality. As one Island executive said, it "forces you to make an opinion one way or the other" about Melissa. And at least one record chain expressed reservations about the image, almost as if they'd never noticed the content of passion and sensuality in Melissa's work before, but decided to sell the album in their stores anyway.

"She's a very sexual artist," an Island spokesman reminded people. "Maybe it's exploitative, but Melissa is not an exploitative person. You're not dealing with a vixen-type artist here."

But the cover, while perhaps a little provocative, a tease, was only one part of the very elaborately produced CD booklet. Glossy color pictures introduced a new look, decidedly more glamorous Melissa, with a shag haircut and a straightforward look in her eye, alternating those images with grainy portraits of her onstage. It was expensive, and an indication that Island was willing to put real muscle behind the album to break Melissa as a star and make her the top-selling artist she deserved to be.

That was also evident from the postponement of the release date. *Never Enough* was planned to be Melissa's big album, to consolidate all the gains she'd made in the last four years. Both her previous releases had eventually gone platinum, as converts came over to her camp after seeing her in concert or watching her videos on VH1. Those kind of steady sales were rare. If everything could come together on this, then she would be a major act.

As usual, she was more than willing to do her part. A long tour had been booked, but even before that, she was at the convention of the National Association of Recording Merchandisers in New Orleans, pressing the flesh of retail chain executives and performing a short set for them. These were the people who decided how many copies of a new record should be carried in the stores, and how it should be promoted—people who, in effect, pushed the album out the door and into the hands of consumers. Their support would be valuable, and Melissa knew she needed it if this really was to be her breakthrough.

From the first notes, that was what it seemed *Never Enough* could be. The careful roughness of the last two albums had been replaced by a sheen. The guts were still very much there, but it seemed as if she was *really* using the capabilities of the studio for the first time, and polishing her music a little more. Unlike the aborted first album, though, it wasn't using technology for its own sake or a phoney "modern" sound.

One listen and it was obvious that Melissa was stretching herself, challenging herself. Instead of the out-and-out rockers or acoustic funk that had predominated in her work, this showed her moving easily from pop to ballad, and going as far as dance music. It was quite different.

"Ain't It Heavy," which was the first single, rocked as much as anything she'd done, but the descending tones of the chorus invited a singalong. It was, in its way, structured in a sophisticated manner that marked a true coming of age for Melissa. She had taken what she did very well and put it in a pop song format that could appeal to a lot of people—the style that Rod Stewart had once carried off so well.

The track "2001," which came next, caused the greatest surprise among people familiar with Melissa's previous work. With its synthesizers and strong dance beat, it wasn't anything anyone would have immediately associated with her, given that rock 'n' roll and dance music—still seen by many as disco—were at different ends of the musical spectrum.

"I always meant for it to be different, from the moment I started writing it on the road in San Diego," she said. "It started with the guitar hook and I reworked the lyrics a lot. I knew I was stepping out of the emotional relationships I usually write about, and I simply wrote how I feel about the world around me."

And she made it work, playing electric guitar herself on the track, a simple riff in a song that was driven by Lewak's "industrial percussion." Keyboards, which were an important part of the whole album, gave this song its bubbling flavor while carrying much of the instrumental melody. It was an experiment, even more than the rest of the album, and one that easily could have failed. Instead, it became a convincing mix of two genres, something that could work just as easily in the clubs as in concert, and, possibly, even on the charts. The bottom line was that it was *very* commercial.

"Dance Without Sleeping," a ballad whose lyrics seemed to reflect some of her reaction to her father's death, completed a powerful opening trio of songs, with Melissa's voice floating hypnotically above keyboards, almost dreamlike, but still hovering near the edge of rage, grounded only by its huskiness.

With those three songs Melissa had already gone much further stylistically than she'd ever been before. She'd opened up, absorbed some of what was happening in modern music, and incorporated it into her own work, adding other colors and textures, even stepping outside her usual boundaries. If she'd remained within the parameters she'd set, how could she continue to grow as an artist? She needed to view everything in a fresh way.

Even that standard, the slow ballad, was given a new look. "Place Your Hand" was about fear and faith, all stark, empty images, and it needed a stripped-down accompaniment to drive the lyrics home. Adding a cello part over the acoustic twelve-string guitar was inspired arranging. Its mournful, dark tone added some deep color and worked as another voice within the song.

Nor was there any reason why it should be immune from studio trickery, which was exactly what Melissa used on the bridge, the echo kicking it all to a higher level.

Only after establishing these new musical frontiers and illustrating how much she'd grown while she'd been away did Melissa revert to her old style with "Must Be Crazy for Me," an Eagles-like rocker with swaggering, strutting, sexual lyrics, the type of piece that would have fit quite comfortably on her first album, as could "Meet Me in the Back." But even those two enjoyed a greater musical complexity, a maturity of arrangement that hadn't been there earlier.

"The Boy Feels Strange" was as close as she'd ever come to writing a love song addressed to a man. Indeed, that was the way many did see it, making their own assumptions about her. Lyrically, however, it was far more ambiguous, with echoes of the relationship Melissa and her father had lived, the emotions always hidden and unspoken. The fire in the song came not so much from the music, which was muted, as from her charged singing.

That feeling of loss wound even tighter on "Keep It Precious," which built and built as the band created a broad musical backdrop, coming to a sad climax, before dropping into the quiet and simple "The Letting Go"—just Melissa singing and playing piano, completing the small tribute in a stark manner that managed to be both touching and honest without ever verging on the maudlin. Indeed, channeling her feelings, healing the hole in her life, brought out strong lyrical powers, much more than she'd demonstrated in the past.

Good as the songs were, closing the album on such a low note wouldn't have been a good commercial strategy. People appreciated depth and substance, but Melissa's fans also wanted their dose of rock 'n' roll, which was in notably shorter supply on *Never Enough*.

"It's for You" was the perfect finale, written for an audience, with the stage in mind. Listening, it was impossible not to envision it as the climax of the show, the last song of the set, serving as both thank you and farewell, involving the crowd, the volume lowering before coming back for the grand finish and the inevitable bows.

In concert you could stamp and clap and demand an encore. But on CD there was no more. All you could do was go back to the beginning and play it all over again.

By using variety and thought in the song styles and arrangements, Melissa had made her best album to date. Thoughtful, even close to pop (as opposed to out-and-out rock) at times, and managing the difficult feat of sounding contemporary without ever being trendy, it marked a great step forward for her. While still able to sound emotional and committed, she had taken the harshest edge off her voice; it was easier to listen to for many who'd hear it on the radio.

"Ain't It Heavy" was the first single from *Never Enough*, the song that seemed the most obvious, blending the rock of her past with a catchy chorus to create something, as *Entertainment Weekly* agreed, that "recalls the young Rod Stewart—she's got the same brassy warmth." With plenty of radio play, and the video in heavy rotation on VH1, it appeared to be an obvious candidate for the Top 40.

Strangely, though, even as the album sold well right from its release, "Ain't It Heavy" never managed to crack the charts. But for a song that never managed to be a hit, it would have a remarkable life, bringing Melissa her Grammy Award for Best Female Rock Performance the following year, a powerful sign of acceptance that made Melissa realize she finally had broken through. By that time she'd come out publicly as a lesbian, which obviously hadn't affected the judges' decision at all. She was being viewed the way she'd always hoped she would be—for the music she'd made, rather than who she was. And that made her victory especially sweet.

Even the critics who'd expressed some reservations about *Brave and Crazy* appeared to be won over by *Never Enough*. In *Rolling Stone,* Jim Cullen wrote, "Her voice is as passionate as ever but used with greater subtlety than before." While there was "nothing as arresting as 'Bring Me Some Water' . . . taken as a whole, 'Never Enough' represents Etheridge's best work to date." *Entertainment Weekly* pointed out the "broader range of styles" and her voice that invoked "truths lyrics alone can't reach." *People* called it "another triumph, something you could dance or think profound thoughts to . . ." And *Stereo Review* concluded that "overall this is an impressive, fully rounded album . . . helping Etheridge show the full range of her writing and performing skills. A stunner."

It looked like this was going to be the big one. *Never Enough* promised to make her a star of major proportions, not just in the United States, but all over the globe. At home, sales certainly began strongly. Melissa's core of fans were hungry for a new record after such a long wait, and plenty more who'd heard "Ain't It Heavy" or one of the other tracks on the radio were eager to find out more about her music.

And she was eager to be back on the road, playing the new material, and enjoying the adrenaline rush that came with every show, the energy exchanged between performer and audience. Her most extensive tour yet had been set up, starting in May in Portland, Maine, with the North American leg alone running until November, slowly and thoroughly working her way across the continent. Eighteen months had passed since she'd last played to audiences. Her profile had increased gradually, and, Island hoped, was about to take an important leap. She'd graduated to larger theaters, with capacities between two and three thousand. And she was able to sell out a lot of them, particularly on the East Coast. That area had traditionally been strong for her, as had Canada, but now she was able to make the transition from a club act with a strong following to a real concert attraction.

Live, she'd become a real force to be reckoned with. All her years of performing had given her a confidence onstage that had gradually increased over the previous tours. Now, with her strongest backing band ever, she could really rip things up—and she did. On guitar, John Shanks had joined her touring ensemble of Mauricio Fritz Lewak and Kevin McCormick. A songwriter of some fame himself, having penned tunes for Joe Cocker and Bonnie Raitt, among others, McCormick proved the perfect foil for her, making her work harder, pushing her.

"Melissa doesn't do anything halfway," he said. "She has never 'walked' through a show. She's a consummate professional, and what you see onstage is exactly what you see when she's off."

The addition of keyboards helped fill out the sound even more. While they were necessary to be able to play the new material from *Never Enough*, they really did add another dimension, freeing Melissa from much of her rhythm guitar role to be a frontwoman.

She was also happy to give the band opportunities to rearrange her songs, to make them more immediate in a live context.

"Melissa is so much fun to hang out with and to make music with that it's easy," John Shanks continued, "because you feel that you can be yourself and take chances and not feel stifled or feel like you're walking on eggshells. . . . She trusts you enough to allow you to do your best work."

The tour, the band, just *playing* was stimulation enough for her. Often, as they traveled from city to city, Melissa would spend her time in the back of the bus working on new songs. The road helped bring out her creative spirit.

For all the good aspects, though, there was also a down side. She was away from Julie for long stretches, often going more than a month without any real break to see her partner.

It was hard for both of them. But even as Melissa was working on her career, so was Julie. She was just beginning work on her directorial debut, a feature that had been tentatively titled *Teresa's Tattoo*. It was a small, independent production, and she was drafting in friends to work on it. Melissa would be there, of course, playing a lounge singer. k.d. lang had a part. Even Lou Diamond Phillips, Julie's former husband, had agreed to take a role.

Indeed, Melissa and Julie's circle of friends had widened dramatically in the last year, until it seemed as if they knew almost everyone who was up and coming in the entertainment world. Ellen Degeneres, Brad Pitt, Jeff Goldblum, Laura Dern, k.d. lang, even Elton John had been guests at their home. It wasn't exactly a typical musician's list of acquaintances. Without even going public, Melissa and Julie had become quite the celebrity lesbian couple.

In some ways, though, life was quite difficult for Julie. Melissa, after all, was a known face. She'd sold millions of records, played all over the world, but not many people knew who Julie Cypher was, or what she did.

"There was a period before I got my first movie made . . . where it was hard for me to be with Melissa because she was doing exactly what she wanted to do professionally," Julie admitted later. "I was just hanging on, tagging along with no purpose in my life."

Maybe that feeling was inevitable, since one of the partners was further along in her career than the other. It wasn't exactly jealousy or resentment, just a simple statement of frustration that things weren't moving as fast as Julie might have liked. And even when

Teresa's Tattoo was complete, it would still take her some time to find a distributor for it.

Part of the love Julie and Melissa shared was mutual respect. They each had their work. They believed in each other, and in themselves.

One thing they understood was that they lived relatively privileged lives. A Spanish-style house in the hills looking down on Los Angeles, behind high walls with an elaborate security system. A pool, a hot tub, waxed wood floors—they'd come a long way from Kansas and Texas.

While Melissa might have earned most of the money to pay for these things, that didn't make them hers; it was decidedly *theirs.* They were a couple completely committed to each other, as much if not more so than any husband and wife with a place in the suburbs. Many of their dreams and aspirations were exactly the same.

"I intend to grow old, fat, and happy with Julie," was the way Melissa put things, and Julie added, "We're a normal, boring couple. We check the grocery list like anyone."

While they had many things in common with other couples, there was one large difference. Melissa didn't commute to an office every day. She was a musician, and when she went on the road, it wasn't like a salesman who'd be back with his family on the weekend. She was gone for a month or more at a stretch, crisscrossing America or in some foreign country, making people believe in her words. It was a world that was almost impossible to explain; endless stretches of inactivity, staring out as countryside rushed past the bus, keying up for those two hours in a day that made it worthwhile, as the lights came up and the audience roared. Melissa had to prepare herself for that night after night. Her reputation, quite justly earned, was that she always gave everything to the audience, and she never wanted to let anybody down. They'd paid their money to see *her.*

On the *Never Enough* tour, she made certain plenty of people had a chance to see what she could do. Had she chosen to limit herself to the larger markets, it could have been over much sooner. But on the back of this record, she had a real chance to become part of the national musical consciousness, someone people would want to see again, whose album they'd feel driven to buy. So she took her show everywhere, beyond the primary markets and into the heartland—Toledo, Spokane—cities all too often ignored by the huge names. Melissa wasn't too proud to stop and play there. Like an evangelist, she had a message for them, and it was in her music.

All the work paid off. Neither "Ain't It Heavy" nor "2001" became hit singles, but *Never Enough* stayed well placed in the American charts for several months, and even gave Melissa her best-selling record yet in England, climbing to number 56. Maybe it wasn't the smash everyone had hoped for, but the showing was more than enough to leave Melissa well established as a very strong attraction. So, as she concluded the tour with two sold-out shows in Chicago, at the Chicago theater ten days before Christmas, 1992, she was able to think she'd done well. While some foreign dates remained in 1993, she had pushed *Never Enough* as much as she could. It had sold enough to bring in a third platinum disc, this one in well under a year. Everything was moving along.

If there was any one disappointment, it was that the singles hadn't sold. "Ain't It Heavy" had seemed to have *hit* written all over it. It had received plenty of airplay. But somehow people just hadn't gone out and spent their money on it. The same was true for both "2001" and "Dance Without Sleeping." She just wasn't able to crack that last barrier, the Top 40.

By the time Melissa went back to Los Angeles for some well-earned rest and recuperation, things were changing politically in America. For the first time since 1976, a Democrat had been elected to the White House. There was a promise of more liberal times ahead, and an acceptance of all kinds of people, including gay men and lesbians. The mood of the entire nation seemed to be shifting to the left.

k.d. lang had already come out in early summer 1992, during an interview with *The Advocate,* a magazine that had decided not to interview Melissa in 1991 because she refused to answer questions about her sexuality. "She didn't want to be asked about her relationship with her girlfriend," recalled then editor-in-chief Glen Yarborough. "And we just said, 'You know, an *Advocate* interview is about sexuality, it's about privacy, and it's about issues of disclosure. All of those things play into every interview we do.' So we just sort of said, 'No, we're not going to interview you.' "

There had been no massive backlash against k.d. In fact, she'd experienced almost the opposite reaction. For a long time many people had suspected that she was a lesbian; to have that confirmed brought a few nods, but no outcry. And *Ingenue,* which appeared at the time the interview had been published, rapidly became her best-selling album to date.

Melissa and k.d. were good friends, and had spent some time together. In fact, Melissa admitted, "k.d. lang turned me into a vegetarian. I stayed with her for a couple of weeks, and since then I've been unable to touch meat."

She'd observed and heard all the things that had happened since k.d. had come out, and knew that nothing bad had occurred. The world hadn't crumbled. It was enough to raise questions in her own mind. Should she come out? Was it time?

Quite naturally, it was a hard decision to make. It was something that would affect her whole life. Her audience was very different from lang's. Some of her fans might be less open-minded. If they made up a big enough number, her career could be over, and she'd end up back in the women's bars, entertaining patrons for tips again.

Discretion proved to be the better part of valor. She wanted people to know the truth about her—honesty was a big part of her Kansas makeup—but at the same time it scared her. She set deadlines, telling one journalist that if "Dance Without Sleeping" flopped as a single, she'd come out, because it would be obvious she'd never manage a hit single. And if the song *was* a hit, she'd also come out, because she'd have leaped that final barrier.

The single appeared and vanished without reaching the charts, but Melissa didn't come out. In so many ways that was understandable. It was a decision that was almost impossible to make rationally, to say "Now I'm ready." k.d. lang's coming out had happened on the spur of the moment. Indeed, afterward, she'd called her record company and said, "I think I just came out to *The Advocate.*" Their reaction? "Oh, shit."

Sooner or later it would happen. Melissa *would* come out. That much appeared inevitable. She was in a committed, stable relationship, happy with her lover, herself, and her career. k.d. had proven that a woman could announce she was a lesbian and still do well—very well, it seemed, as k.d. ended up nominated for five Grammys, including Best Album and Best Female Vocalist.

Melissa, too, found herself with a nomination, in the Best Rock Vocal Performance, Female category, for "Ain't It Heavy." Her first nomination since 1989, when "Bring Me Some Water" had failed to win, went some way to compensate for the fact that it hadn't been a hit.

While coming out weighed heavily on her mind, there were plenty of other matters to occupy Melissa. Christmas needed to be celebrated, she needed to unwind after so many months of traveling, to get to know Julie again, and have a life at home.

She also had to look ahead. The cycle of *Never Enough* was almost over, which meant she had to begin thinking about her next record. The gains she'd made meant that waiting another two and a half years for her next release was impractical. It *needed* to be sooner than that. Audiences could be notoriously fickle, and who could say when the next Melissa Etheridge might happen along and explode on the scene?

That meant she'd have to make decisions soon, about songs,

players, studios, producers. She had material she'd written on the road, but was it all good enough to record and release? Did she want to change her sound again? *Never Enough* had been an experiment that had paid off, to some extent. It had brought more people into the fold with its openness and commerciality. Did she want to continue in that vein? Should she handle the production chores again, or bring in an outsider who could look at things objectively and offer suggestions that might never occur to her?

They all had to be considered. And they were all her responsibility.

$\mathscr{S}$EVEN

$\mathscr{M}$elissa couldn't have known it, but as she pondered all those problems, she was about to embark on what was the pivotal year of her life: 1993 would be, without a doubt, a turning point when everything came together. Was it fate, was it karma? That was impossible to say. But it was definitely an important time for Melissa Etheridge.

It began with a bang on January 20, in Washington, D.C. Melissa and Julie had been invited to attend the Triangle Ball in celebration of President Clinton's inauguration that day. It was just one of many parties around town, but this one, organized by the Gay and Lesbian Alliance, had a special significance. After twelve years of Republican administrations, there was finally someone in the White House who appeared to be gay-friendly. The National Press Club was packed with two thousand people to show exactly what "The New Gay Power" meant.

It was an evening of joy, laughter, and more especially revelation. The podium was filled with celebrities addressing the crowd. Cassandra Peterson, better known as television's horror movie queen of ceremonies, Elvira, announced, "You know, I'm not a lesbian . . . but I could certainly be talked into being one tonight." The hall filled with cheers.

Then k.d. lang spoke, telling everyone, "You know the best thing I ever did was to come out." There was more raucous applause. As k.d. moved aside, Melissa stood by the microphone, filled with the spirit of the evening.

"My sister k.d. lang has been such an inspiration," she said. "She did the greatest thing I've ever seen this year. I'm very proud to say I've been a lesbian all my life."

She'd done it. She'd finally come out. All the months of wavering were over. k.d. grabbed and hugged her, and the crowd went berserk.

"I walked back, and Julie looked at me, and I just kind of went, 'I think I just came out.' "

The passion of the night had overtaken her, and she'd shown *everyone* the real Melissa, the lesbian all-American girl. That was fine for the evening, when she was full of euphoria. But the next morning, in the cold light of day, it was still there. In black and white: "The next day it was in the *New York Post:* BUTCH ROCKER MELISSA ETHERIDGE COMES OUT."

"I always intended to do it," she explained later in *The Advocate*, "but I didn't know when or where. I just couldn't dodge it anymore. I felt like I was lying, and my music is so much about the truth."

Since she was a public figure, it wasn't too long before the articles began appearing in magazines about her sexuality. And now she was happy to talk about it. Having spilled the secret, it was time to be completely open about things.

k.d. had been influential in helping Melissa to say the words. When she was considering coming out, k.d. had asked for Melissa's advice.

"So I'm telling her, 'Go for it! Go for it!' And she does it. And I'm kind of standing there going, 'Well, I should practice what I preach.' And she never suggested or pressured me or said that I should."

Now she had. It was scary, wondering what would happen. She told *The Advocate:*

"You think there's some big black hole you're going to fall into and that all of a sudden people who have loved you all your life aren't going to love you anymore. . . . In record-business terms, my exact fear was that I had been embraced by rock radio—which was unheard-of for a woman of any sexual orientation. So just as a woman, I was already breaking ground. I was dealing with that and thinking, 'OK, if I come out, how many stations are going to drop me?' It's another version of the same fear: being dropped, being abandoned. . . . Mine is heartland music. My audiences are very mixed. So I worried, 'If I come out, will it make me strange?' "

But fear and reality proved to be two completely different things. If any stations at all stopped playing her music, they were too few and far between to have even been noticed.

Her record company remained firmly behind her, as Matt Stringer, senior vice president of marketing at Island, told *Billboard.*

"I see her coming out as positive," he announced. "Her music is all about being honest, so it made sense for her to choose not to hide this part of who she is. There was a brief discussion [at the label] about its potential impact, and everyone felt it had to be a nonissue."

On a more personal level, Melissa lost no friends or family over coming out.

"When it was in *People* magazine, I called [my mother], and I said, 'Well, Mom, it's in *People* magazine. So if there are any relatives far away that I don't know about that might call you and give you a hassle, I just want to let you know.' And she's like, 'If they can't handle it, that's their problem.' . . . And the relatives have been great."

Still, it put her in a unique situation. She was the only out lesbian rock 'n' roll artist around. The reaction to her coming out had been quiet. But what would it mean for the future? How would it affect the new album that was due later in the year? Would anyone play it? Would anyone buy it? The only way she'd get the answers would be when it was released.

The first wave of publicity about her sexuality blew up and calmed down, and Melissa could take the time to catch her breath.

"Coming out is such a personal thing," she reflected later. "So much personal baggage and issues go on behind it. Maybe if I hadn't had such a good experience with my family, perhaps I would not have had as much confidence when it came to coming out to the world."

Certainly it helped that she and Julie enjoyed such a solid relationship. It was a foundation, security for a whole life. It left her less scared to stand in the bright spotlight of the media knowing she had someone there with her, beside her, there for her all the time.

After anticipating the worst, Melissa found the best—a great deal of sympathy. So many people already knew, or suspected, that she was a lesbian that her words came more as confirmation than surprise. For the most part, the media treated the news kindly, bringing out the human side rather than searching for any lurid sensationalism. And that was the way it should have been.

There was also an irony, in that some of the journalists who'd previously been asking about her sexual preferences were now coming out to *her*.

"There were all these journalists," she remembered, "who would come out to me. They're not out, but they felt like they could tell me."

One immediate effect of Melissa's declaration was to raise her public profile. All too often musicians only sit down and talk to the press when they have a new record to promote—in other words, when *they* want to spend time talking. Coming out, though, had made her public property. She became, within a matter of months, music's second lesbian after k.d. lang, or, as Melissa put it, "I'm the Al Gore of lesbians."

Now, with the not-so-secret news out, it was easier for Melissa to live her life exactly the way she wanted. There was nothing to hide. She didn't have to constantly monitor her words or her actions. She could be who she really was.

Which is why, when she arrived at the Grammy Awards ceremony in March, she was holding Julie's hand. It wasn't a gesture of defiance, simply another couple entering together. If they were going to turn heads because they were both women, well, that was the way things were going to be.

It turned out to be night of the lesbians. Melissa had been nominated for one award. k.d. was up for five. Each of them walked away with a Grammy. k.d.'s was for Best Female Vocal Performance, for her *Ingenue* album, while Melissa received the award for Best Rock Vocal Performance, Female, for the song so many had loved, but which never became a hit, "Ain't It Heavy." In her acceptance speech she was able to dedicate the award to her father, as well as to thank someone she wouldn't have been able to publicly acknowledge a month earlier—Julie, her lover.

With the awards out of the way, and the statue shining on the mantlepiece, it was time for Melissa to begin work on her new record. More than any of the others, this one would be a leap of faith. It could go either of two ways: flop horribly, since everyone now knew all about her life, or be the biggest thing she'd ever done, boosted by her honesty and the Grammy.

Time would tell.

While Melissa was working on that, Julie was completing *Teresa's Tattoo*, spending her days in a different studio, or an editing suite, completely absorbed in her own project.

"It is hard," Melissa commented, "because there are two very competitive, seriously creative people here. It's fucking hard. . . .

When she was making her . . . movie, I was making my . . . album, saying, 'Where are you? You're usually in the studio listening to me?' Suddenly I had to play wife: I had to feed the dog every day."

Their conflicting schedules undoubtedly created stress, but it was nothing they couldn't handle. The work was something Julie really needed to do. For the three years they'd been together, she'd largely lived in Melissa's shadow. It wasn't as if she was a dilettante filmmaker, either; she'd had a professional career established well before the two ever met.

So working on *Teresa's Tattoo* was vitally important. It gave Julie a sense of self, of contributing *something*. And when she'd completed it, she said, "Now that the film is finished and I have this sense of accomplishment, it's much easier for me to tag along, to be on the bus."

The film wasn't a big production for one of the studios. Written by Georgie Huntington, it wasn't even the kind of independent film that could ever see widespread release. Originally titled *Arduous Moon*, *Teresa's Tattoo* was a strange farce starring Adrienne Shelly, in two roles, and C. Thomas Howell, with cameos by Julie's ex, Lou Diamond Phillips, as a janitor, Tippi Hedren, Mare Winningham, Keifer Sutherland, k.d. lang as an unhappy customer in a restaurant, and Melissa tickling the ivories as the performer in the piano bar (she also supplied all the music for the film).

While few people saw it in theaters, it remains available on video, and it did establish Julie as someone who could write and direct an entire film, leaving the way open for her current work on another independent feature.

As soon as she came out, the amount of mail that Melissa received grew enormously, not only from individuals—mostly young women—but also from politically oriented groups. Her new public status as an open lesbian, coupled with her fame, meant that plenty of people wanted to make demands on her time. She became a member of the advisory board for Artists for a Hate-Free America, which worked nationally with grassroots organizations to fight all types of antigay legislation and initiatives, and agreed to perform at a fundraiser for them. She also supported Don Henley's work trying to preserve historic Walden Woods, agreeing to play at another fundraiser for that. ABC television asked her to work with them on "In a New Light '93," a prime-time news show intended to heighten AIDS awareness. On a local level she worked with the Shanti organization in Los Angeles, giving help and support to people with AIDS. As if all that wasn't enough when Melissa had her own work to do, "I've been asked to do every gay parade in the country."

Activism, the willingness to actually get out and do something that might make a positive change, was important to her. That meant becoming involved, on some level, in politics.

"It's something I care about," she explained. "It's important to me whether this state [California] passes a law where a teacher who suspects someone of being an illegal alien can turn them in. This is my state. This is my society. And if my vote can make a difference to whether that happens or not, that's important to me."

Prior to the 1992 election she'd used her name to campaign for Bill Clinton, "because I felt like he represented change, and he was embracing it and all for it."

In return, when she and Julie toured the White House in 1994, they were invited to meet the President.

"Next thing, we're in the Oval Office chatting with Bill," Julie remembered. It was an experience that left even the normally voluble Melissa tongue-tied.

"I said, 'You know, I've always wanted to tell you, if I ever had the opportunity, that I used to spend my summers in Arkansas, and it means a lot to me, knowing the dreams I had as a kid, another kid who grew up in Arkansas grew up to be President.' "

"That's what you would have said," Julie corrected her.

"No, that's what I said. So he says, 'Oh, your mother is from Arkansas? Where does she live?' And I could not remember. And he realizes that I'm losing it. I choked."

"She turns around and says, 'Help me out here,'" Julie laughed.

It was one of the few moments in her life that had left Melissa awed, and, according to Julie, unable to recall exactly what she'd said. It was, in its own small way, a historic meeting: the President of the United States of America having a personal discussion with an out, avowedly lesbian rock 'n' roll singer and her lover. As much as anything, it was a sign of the new administration's acceptance of different lifestyles.

Melissa was also a vocal supporter of the pro-choice movement, although, as she pointed out, "it's so interesting being a lesbian and knowing that I don't have to worry about that. You know, abortion is not even an issue with me. But a woman's choice is so fierce to me." She had strong feelings about the issue itself, but also for the issues of personal freedom it represented. "What's next? Well, gee, you can't wear your skirt above your knee? Where does it stop? I don't think people should judge and take that away from someone. Everyone has their own battles and their own spirituality and their own issues. You can't govern that."

Celebrities are often asked to be the figureheads or spokespeople for various organizations and movements. All too often their name or photograph means little more than token involvement. In Melissa's case, though, her sexuality had made her into a political figure. That was impossible to avoid. In an era where the increasing volume of the conservative and religious right continued to attack homosexuality as evil, and tried to help states pass initiatives ensuring that gays would end up treated as little more than second-class citizens, she found herself pitched into the middle of the battle, like it or not. As her time and energy allowed, she was happy to participate—which had led to her activities with Artists for a

Hate-Free America, a job she took very seriously, as well as Shanti (which thanked her with an award in 1995) and the Lifebeat Concerts, yearly events that raised money for AIDS care and research. These were the issues that really touched her heart. She knew that she was lucky to enjoy the life she did, to have a steady lover, a very comfortable home in the Hollywood Hills, and a privileged life. She felt it was her responsibility to give something back, to make some small difference.

After all the media attention surrounding her coming out and then winning a Grammy, it was now time to fully focus her thoughts on a new record. The songs were written and ready to be recorded.

Kevin McCormick, her longtime bass player, and the man who'd coproduced her first three albums, was only able to work on some of the album, due to prior commitments, and he wasn't able to help with the production. That meant she needed to draft in a fresh set of ears and an objective mind to help her produce this one. She finally picked Hugh Padgham, whose work in the control room had helped the Police, among others, achieve their phenomenal success.

Mauricio Fritz Lewak remained to play drums, although he had stopped touring with her. The rest of the core of the recording band was made up of session players, Waddy Wachtel on guitar (whose work had added a great deal to her debut); Scott Thurston, back again to play keyboards, as he'd done on all her other albums; and both Pino Palladino, the British musician, and David Sutton filling in on bass.

Even before she set foot in the studio, Melissa had a title picked out: *Yes I Am*.

"When I wrote the song 'Yes I Am,' I said, 'Oh, my gosh. I want to title an album that.' "

Obviously, there was a certain way many people would take the title, and Melissa acknowledged that.

"Well, I knew when I titled it that I'd come out. So I'd hoped that it would be 'Are you gay? Yes, you are.' But I also hoped it would encompass all the other things."

Specifically, though, it was "a romantic song. It's about a commitment. It's also about obsession."

And it was about Julie, although that was true of much of the material she was recording. If *Never Enough* had dealt in great part with her late father and looked back on the relationship they'd shared during his life, this one was going to be very much based in the present.

" 'Yes I Am' is one of the first love songs I ever wrote," Melissa admitted. "I thought at the time, OK, I'm really gonna say I want to be everything to you. I want to be your passion, your promise, everything. I want to be your now, your future, your end. And that's what love can lead you to."

So while the album continued several of the same themes as much of Melissa's previous work, the songs this time were much more closely focused, and more specifically autobiographical.

" 'Come to My Window' was written when I was away from Julie physically. You know when you are away from someone physically, and you have that communication breakdown? You're thinking, she's not listening to what I'm saying; I'm not listening to what she's saying. . . . The song is about that point. It's as if I'm saying: 'You don't know how far I'd go to ease this. With the fear that I'm feeling, I will leave my job and fly home just to reach you, to make sure that you're OK.' "

Even though many of the words dealt with her own relationship, and her sexuality was known, Melissa continued to make the object of her lyrical desires a genderless "You," a fact that surprised a lot of people. After all, she had nothing to hide now. Couldn't she just have addressed them to a woman?

"I write from a genderless place," she answered. "I don't think I will ever write or sing 'I love *her*.' I like that my music reaches not just gay but straight fans—men and women both."

At the same time, she didn't completely eliminate the possibility of writing a song "about Julie, saying how much she means to me"; however, if it happened, it would occur in its own time.

So Melissa spent much of the early spring driving her black Jaguar XKE from home to A&M Studios—which had been her recording base for a few years now—every day.

Yes I Am would be a return to basics. *Never Enough* had been constructed slowly, like a building, to be state of the art. It had been wonderfully clean in its sound. Now Melissa wanted to go back to the rock 'n' roll dirtiness of her first couple of records. All the basic tracks were recorded live in the studio, the band all together, sparking off each other, doing it over and over again in search of that elusive perfect take, with everything recorded in an analog format before being mixed to digital, to give the sound of "real music slapping against tape." The experimentation of *Never Enough* had been interesting, a diversion Melissa had wanted and needed to explore. It had given her a sense of growth, and of the possibilities in her own music. And it had given her a fuller, richer sound that she'd continue to use. It had also shown her that her musical heart belongs quite firmly to rock 'n' roll. It was the music she listened to, loved to play, and that came most naturally to her.

As she worked on the record, she knew in her mind that it felt right, that she was doing the best work of her career. All the pieces, it seemed, were coming together perfectly. The record label had believed that *Never Enough* would be her breakthrough, and they'd been wrong. It hadn't won her a mass audience. But Melissa felt *this* would be the one, even if she didn't hear a Top 40 single among the tracks.

"There were times I wished I could write a hit," she said. "But you can't just sit down and write one. I can't. All I can do is write what's in me, and try to craft it as well as I can. There's not a song on any of my albums that was contrived to be a hit."

The recording complete, she left Padgham to finish the mixing, and returned to the place where her music came most alive—the road. After long, grueling days in the studio, it was refreshing to be able to present complete songs, and see how the new material worked in front of an audience. And since it was only for a few dates, she had the pleasure of performing without all the grind of endless travel.

In her shows, Melissa discovered another way that coming out had liberated her.

"I can now do all the classic seventies songs that I love," she said. "Springsteen songs like 'Thunder Road' . . . now I can sing that. The classic rock songs were written about women, and I always felt I couldn't do them because it would make people feel awkward. But now people are in on it and appreciate it. I do 'Maggie May.' People love it."

Her brief summer tour climaxed on Labor Day weekend with the Walden Woods concert, organized by Don Henley to raise funds that would keep Thoreau's historic site pristine. Fans gathered at Foxborough Stadium in Massachusetts to hear Henley (whom Melissa knew, having contributed backing vocals to his "New York Minute" a few years before), Elton John, Sting, Aerosmith, and Melissa.

"Steven Tyler came up to me," she recalled, ". . . gave me a big hug and said, 'You are just fabulous.' . . . I actually made the mistake of saying that I felt like the girl on the block, and Don Henley called me, concerned that he had committed some feminist crime."

What she'd said, though, merely stated the obvious, that rock 'n' roll remained a boys' club. For Melissa to be accepted among the "big boys" (and by career longevity and record sales, the other stars very definitely represented an elite) meant she'd broken down some barriers that had stood for a long time.

Were there any other women in line behind her yet? Not really. She'd been born on a cusp, just young enough to have missed the baby boom, and too old to be part of the so-called Generation X. She was a rock 'n' roller "who is proud of that fact in an age when rock is considered old and incredible rock 'n' roll artists want to be called alternative." She was referring to the up-and-coming women, the Liz Phairs and Julianna Hatfields, who were careful to steer clear of the mainstream. So Melissa was standing out there, all on her own. She was, quite literally, the female face of rock 'n' roll.

EIGHT

From the day of its release in October 1993, *Yes I Am* caught the imagination of the record-buying public. It was as if America had finally caught up with the music that Melissa was making, even though, in essence, not much had changed from her first album. It was down-the-line rock 'n' roll, the song was always the thing, and her voice was almost consumed by its own passion.

From the first notes it was obvious that Hugh Padgham had achieved a specific sound, full of presence, as Melissa's twelve-string Ovation kicked off "I'm The Only One" before a blues beat took the song over, and layered electric instruments managed to sound thick and spare at the same time. Typically for Melissa's songs, the lead guitar played an obbligato behind her vocals, rather than over them, only taking a short solo. Her voice had the thick raspiness that had characterized her best work; it was blues-rock of the highest order, with a strong chorus—the type of piece that wasn't exactly fashionable in the nineties, but that still held a lot of appeal.

"If I Wanted To" worked similarly, fleshing the sound out with keyboards, and working around a chorus that consisted of the title, building through the verse to explode and free itself.

Much the same was true of "Come to My Window," which was, perhaps, the best song Melissa had recorded, melodically sophisticated, using jangly REM-style guitars behind the chorus to drive it home. As was often the case, the lyrics were about romantic and sexual obsession, but couched in such an engaging melody that their intensity almost passed the listener by.

Melissa had never felt herself restricted by the three-minute, pop-song format. Everything she recorded was, in its own way, an epic, with its own sense of ebb and flow, and she'd always let the material stretch out to gain the full impact, rather than concern herself with editing for easier radio play.

"Silent Legacy" was typical of that, running more than five minutes, building on an acoustic beginning, adding instruments, and culminating in a spiraling guitar solo that blew the lid off the intensity.

This definitely wasn't an album where many ballads would have sounded at home. With an overall feel that was sweaty and quite sexual, anything soft and gentle would have been utterly out of place. As close as the record came was "I Will Never Be the Same"; it might have been softer and gentler, but it still had the beat and the heat, and a slide guitar solo that brought to mind the Rolling Stones' "Exile on Main Street"—as did much of "Yes I Am." It was more feel than content, strong rhythm, a thick backbeat, and songs that didn't know how to do anything except rock. While on her previous work the lead guitar had mostly taken a role of coloring and filling out the arrangements, here it was given some space, let out for short solos, never self-indulgent, but always incisive contributions, which helped push the songs even farther down that rock 'n' roll path. *Yes I Am* appeared to be the culmination of everything Melissa had done before, refined, confident, simply and powerfully presented, a record that knew it was good and dared you to say otherwise.

Perhaps the weakest track was the one with the most explicit social commentary, "All American Girl," which peeked into the unhappy lives of three different women to a tune that was, by her standards, more or less a throwaway. However, it served to focus the spotlight on the title track that followed, one of Melissa's most intense performances, quite explicit in its promises, hopes, and desires. It didn't need a furious beat to make its message obvious, simmering at midtempo, the instrumentation deliberately spare, letting Melissa's voice carry the weight of the tune. It was all too easy to imagine it being sung in concert, bodies swaying as the audience joined in on the chorus.

"Resist" almost took a turn toward the New Wave of the 1970s, its opening riff naggingly reminiscent of Talking Heads' "Life During Wartime," and none the worse for that, before smoothly shifting gears into a neat little pop song. It might never have stood alone as a great piece, but within the context of the album it worked perfectly well.

A nagging riff was also the centerpiece of "Ruins," underpinned by Kevin McCormick's bass playing, before opening out in the chorus as Scott Thurston's synthesizer filled out the chords. Without reverting to the white-girl chicken scratch rhythms that had characterized some of the material from *Brave and Crazy*, it still managed to add the funk element Melissa had liked to include in her work, mixing it seamlessly with pop.

With Melissa, it was impossible to forget that she was influenced by Bruce Springsteen, and on "Talking to My Angel" it really came through, employing the sustained keyboard chords under the melody that had become so common on the Boss's recent work: the simple, stripped-down, big drum beat that acted more as anchor than propellor, and a tune that washed over the listener, with the accordian of James Fearnley, from the Pogues, adding color. Lyrically it was inspired by the churches that had been among the many places she had played when she was young. "I was constantly around all these religious images, and to me angels exist . . . I feel we are definitely guided and helped, and I'm always referring to them in my work."

Overall, *Yes I Am* stood as a guided tour around twenty years of rock 'n' roll as seen through Melissa's eyes and unified in her voice. There was plenty on the album that sounded vaguely familiar and comfortable, not only to her longtime fans, but to anyone who was familiar with rock. The beauty was in the way it had all been put together. Melissa had never claimed to be a great innovator; her gift was writing and singing powerful songs, and these were the best of her career, drawing on the past, on the music she'd loved for so long, taking its feel, occasionally even its sound, and making that completely her own, putting herself in direct line with the great rock 'n' rollers.

It was very American music, and quite explicitly Midwestern, even though there was only one lyrical reference to the heartland. But it still captured the spirit of a place and time, the hopes and the fears. Melissa was from the Midwest. California might have been her home for twelve years, but there was no escaping the past; it was in her blood. She just summed up what people felt, their aspirations and dreams, their desires and wishes, and put it to the beat they'd been hearing from car radios all their lives. With *Yes I Am* she somehow tapped perfectly into the zeitgeist.

Nationally, radio picked up on "I'm The Only One," the lead-off track, and soon it was filling the AAA (Adult Album Alternative) airwaves, along with the classic rock stations who'd been her longtime supporters. Then the video went into heavy rotation on VH1. At that point it would have seemed the logical choice for a single. Instead, Island Records went with "Come to My Window," which managed something she'd never been able to do before: to crack the Top 40, rising to 22 as the year ended.

In *Stereo Review, Yes I Am* was seen to be "at times reminiscent of a good midperiod Stones album . . . a hard-charging, heart-on-sleeve quest for the state of determined self-affirmation embodied in its title." *Entertainment Weekly* felt it to be more intimate than most of the male rock being produced with "a darkness that's very appealing" and, of course, Melissa's "haunted rasp of a voice . . ."

Real promotion of the album had barely begun yet. Melissa had played a few select dates, but the real touring had still to begin. Already she had one hit single, the album was in the Top 30, and her videos were receiving almost constant airplay on VH1. It looked as though 1994 would be the year of Melissa Etheridge.

Chris Blackwell, the head of Island, and the man who'd signed her, was overjoyed at the success.

"She has character and ability, which is so rare," he said. "In a way, she is starting on part two of her career right now. Part one was getting to this point. I have no doubt that she will be the biggest female rock performer in the world."

Melissa herself was able to revel in the fact that, by just continuing to do what she did so well—rock—she'd eventually be able to find the larger audience she knew existed for her music.

"I just do what I do and hope that people will discover it along the way," she said. "This is strong and straightforward rock 'n' roll. I think that I've built a real momentum with this album," and adding elsewhere, "I've just focused on doing what feels natural and comfortable. It's hard to know what will happen, and I have never wanted to compromise myself. . . . The sweetness is in having success with something you really believe in."

She'd finally become the major star she always hoped to be, with another hit album, a hit single. Things could only grow from here as she prepared to spend a year on the road.

"It's been a long time since a female rock artist has broken through to this extent," commented the vice president of music programming at VH1, Lee Chesnut. "You almost have to go back to someone like Pat Benatar."

But while Pat could sing, and had proved popular on the young MTV network, there had always seemed something manufactured about her work; it could have come off a songwriting assembly line. Melissa, as America was finally comprehending, was the real thing.

She delivered the goods, no-holds-barred, out-and-out rock. She didn't have to carefully work in images and emotions that would appeal to the blue-collar listeners; they were a natural, integral part of her music.

The only real question was why had *this* album caught fire, as opposed to her earlier releases? Part of the answer had to be visibility. During 1993 her name had become a familiar one, between the articles regarding her coming out and winning the Grammy. Some people, undoubtedly, wanted to discover what a lesbian rock 'n' roll singer would sound like. For others, the Grammy had been the final seal of approval.

Perhaps the real reason, though, was that Melissa had finally achieved critical mass. Over the course of the five years since *Melissa Etheridge* had been released, she'd played endless shows around the world. Her albums had sold very respectably, not enough to push her into the superstar class, but steadily nonetheless. She'd built a strong fan base, one that was constantly growing. Her music might not have been for everybody—and certainly not those who traveled the "alternative" route—but the people who became converted to her cause were fervent followers.

Eventually all that had to pay off, and it was *Yes I Am* that was reaping the harvest. *Never Enough* had been every bit as commercial, possibly even more so with its stylistic diversity, but now, finally, the time was right for Melissa to claim her place in the sun.

"Come to My Window" peaked at 22. Breaking the barrier of the Top 20 would have been wonderful, but there would be plenty more opportunities for that to happen.

The album continued to make its own climb up the charts. All too often, after an initial surge of radio and video play, sales of a record tail off, and its day is over. With *Yes I Am* that just didn't seem to be happening. It stayed hot. Melissa's songs kept receiving airplay. Demand at the record stores remained constant. She'd become the unofficial queen of VH1.

And it was only just becoming time to tour and promote the

album. For the first time in a number of years, Melissa would be starting out as an opening act. Having been offered the chance to join Sting on tour, she wasn't about to turn that opportunity down. It would expose her to a new audience, one which, hopefully, would quickly start buying her records.

The experience wasn't completely without its traumas, though. As the tour opened in Florida, a man walked to the stage and put a religious tract at Melissa's feet—a rather obvious reference to her sexuality, and one that left her temporarily flustered.

"It was a 'God Will Save Your Life' kind of book. But I realized later that he might have put that up there anyway just for my being a rock star."

That, however, proved to be one of the only negative reactions to coming out that she'd experience from audiences. She won over the crowds (and the Top 40 radio programmers who'd come to see the headliner), and even Sting himself, who brought her out every night to duet on "Every Breath You Take."

"It was his first encore, so he'd taken off his shirt," Melissa recalled, showing she wasn't completely blind to male charms. "He's so beautiful. I just wanted to touch him. . . . I did, a couple of times. I appreciate beauty in all its forms—male and female, all energies."

By the end of February those dates were complete, and it was time for the first leg of her own lengthy world tour, which would run until the end of June, with Matthew Sweet as the opening act. This saw Melissa well and truly established in the theater circuit, selling out venues that just a couple of years earlier would have been well beyond her reach.

And *Yes I Am* stayed hot on the album charts. It had broken the Top 20 finally, rising to 16, with no signs of dropping anytime soon. Sales had already passed the one million mark, giving Melissa another platinum disc for her collection. Everything really was coming together.

As "Come to My Window" began to fade as a single, it was replaced by "I'm The Only One," which had already become a radio favorite as an album track. It would prove to be one of *the* songs of the summer and fall, just failing to make the Top 10—a remarkable achievement for a time when the hit parade was almost exclusively country or hip-hop—and having the legs to last in the charts until almost the end of 1994.

Melissa's visibility was increasing almost on a daily basis. During July she opened a series of concerts for the re-formed Eagles in the South and Midwest. Not only was it great timing to keep the album and single alive, it was wonderful exposure to an audience that would love her—the baby boomers who'd come out to relive the memories of their youth.

Her live performance had always been outstanding, but on this tour it was something special. She was finally receiving the rewards she'd worked so long and hard to earn. If anything, coming out seemed to have brought real success. She was happy, and giving the music everything she had at every show. The audience fed her with energy, and she gave it back to them. It was all part of the karma that was propelling her life that year. It was, she firmly believed, all due to having told the truth about herself; honesty paid.

"*Yes I Am*, the album that came out after I did, is my most successful album so far; my work has been more successful than it ever was before—my tours, everything," she said. "On a spiritual level I believe that confronting the fear of coming out loosened up and freed all other aspects of my life. I just think that when you do that for yourself, when you stand up and say 'This is what I am,' then good things come to you. I believe that, and I am totally an example of that."

It was a year of changes. Melissa and Julie sold the house they'd lived in since being together, and bought a larger one, still in the Hollywood hills. Built in 1933 in the Spanish hacienda style, it marked a big step upward, with four bedrooms and three thousand square feet of space. By Hollywood standards that might still have been on the small side, but it was more than adequate for their needs. Formerly owned by movie producer Edward R. Pressman, it was supposedly sold for $1.3 million, although Julie later characterized the price as "a fucking lie." Melissa gave up her beloved Jaguar XKE—the lease was up—and began driving a BMW 740i, also in black. All the good things were coming in.

Following her dates with the Eagles, Melissa resumed her own tour, which included a stop between dates at Woodstock '94, the twenty-fifth anniversary of the original festival.

But while the first Woodstock had turned into a huge celebration of the burgeoning hippie culture, the festival to end all festivals, with free love, drugs, and music—the archetype of sex, drugs, and rock 'n' roll—Woodstock '94 was very much a business venture, with a $30 million budget, and corporate sponsorship from companies like Pepsi, Apple Computer, and Haagen-Dazs. Some of the top performers would receive up to $350,000 for their appearances.

Inevitably, there would be merchandising, almost every item imaginable with the Woodstock '94 logo, advertised in the press, offered on the QVC home shopping channel and on MTV, which gave extensive coverage of the event. Curiously, no one seemed too astonished by all these moves.

"Everyone knows that marketing is part of rock 'n' roll," Melissa said, "and I don't think anybody expects it to be different with Woodstock. That's our culture now."

Melissa found herself on a bill with a massive array of talent, everyone from Nine Inch Nails, Metallica, and Green Day to Peter Gabriel, Traffic, and Bob Dylan. It was, truly, a once-in-a-lifetime occurrence, and the perfect place to pay tribute to one of her great idols, Janis Joplin, who'd been part of the Woodstock generation but hadn't performed at the original festival. The timing, the mood, the place were all right as she wailed into "Piece of my Heart" as if Janis's ghost was possessing her. In a time when music seemed ruled by the accountant's bottom line rather than its content, she, and a few others, managed to revive the idea of liberation and the rebellion that rock 'n' roll had originally been about.

"I kept telling myself not to have any great expectations about Woodstock," she told *Billboard* later. "There was a real possibility that it could have ended up like some horrible corporate thing. From the moment I arrived, I knew that it was larger than life. It was of a scope that reached beyond any of the artists there. . . . I think Woodstock filled something that is lacking today—it was part of a primitive instinct that has not surfaced for some time now."

Woodstock '94 was definitely a high watermark for her in that year, even though it was just one of a seemingly endless string of shows that would run all the way until December, in America and overseas, culminating in a sold-out date at Madison Square Garden—17,530 people in attendance—on December 13, 1994, a magical night when 100 fans from the Melissa Etheridge Information Network fired their lighters together during the emotional "Silent Legacy," enough to start Melissa herself crying.

For the final two months she'd graduated to the place where her music had always seemed aimed—arenas. If Melissa needed any more proof that she'd really arrived, this was it.

Even her hometown of Leavenworth held a Melissa Etheridge Day in November. A new athletic field was dedicated in her father's name, she was honored by the civic dignitaries, and she played once again in the high school auditorium.

"Man, the memories, boom, right back there. It was just . . . a great experience." She even found time to go to the music store where she'd purchased strings and instruments "and my old guitar teacher was still there!"

The fact that as the calendar turned to 1995 *Yes I Am* had sold more than two million copies only furthered that sense of achievement. While no longer in the Top 20, the album remained on the charts, having been lodged there for more than a year, and continued to move over the counter quite steadily.

"We can see this thing being a three million seller before the day is done," an Island spokesman was quoted as saying. "But this is not her *Born in the U.S.A.*—it's her *Born to Run.* We're just getting started."

He didn't realize how true those words would be. *Yes I Am* was just moving into second gear. By the time everything was done, it would end up selling a staggering five million copies, impressive by anyone's standards.

Of course, Melissa had gone out and really worked the record, spending a full year and half touring the world in support of it. The two hit singles made her an even more frequent presence on the radio. VH1 might as well have adopted her, they played her videos so often. But the appearance at Woodstock definitely helped, as did word-of-mouth. More people bought the album, praised it to their friends, who then went out and bought it for themselves. Word-of-mouth was the most potent advertising available. And having become converts, these new fans would see her when she appeared in their towns. It was a spiral.

The hotter she became, the harder it was for Melissa to avoid the public eye. January, when she was supposedly in the middle of a break from touring, resting at home, saw her at the Rock 'n' Roll Hall of Fame for the posthumous induction of Janis Joplin, singing a medley of Janis's most familiar songs, her voice once again capturing the feel of the original.

That same month brought her nominations for two Grammys. For Female Rock Vocal Performance, "Come to My Window" went up against songs by Sheryl Crow, Liz Phair, Sam Phillips, and Bonnie Raitt, and in the Best Rock Song category its competitors were "All Apologies" by Nirvana, Soundgarden's "Black Hole Sun," and "Streets of Philadelphia" by her hero, Bruce Springsteen.

In the latter category, she, along with the Seattle upstarts, never had much chance against the Boss, who took home four awards. But it was Melissa who upset Sheryl Crow's run of luck (Crow won in three other categories, even beating Bruce for Record of the Year). And after the remarkable show of strength "Come to My Window" had shown in the charts, the award was more than justified. It *was* a rock song, and an excellent performance.

It also stood as a consolidation of all Melissa had achieved in the last few years. The Grammys had helped her career in its early days by having her perform on the award show. Her 1993 award had been a boost to her career just as she was entering the superstar arena, and this second award pushed home the fact that she'd really made it to the top. Melissa was grateful, as she noted in her acceptance speech, not only to the judges, but also to everyone who'd helped her along the way.

It seemed as if Melissa was suddenly everywhere on television. Just a few weeks later she was back again on "MTV Unplugged." MTV had always only tacitly accepted her, airing some of her videos, but never giving her the wholehearted shove she'd received from VH1. But she was a natural choice for their "Unplugged" series. The very nature of her music, based around songs and chord changes rather than riffs or rhythms, fitted the format. Most of her writing had been done on an acoustic guitar, anyway. But while so many of the artists brought their full bands along as instrumental support, Melissa took the title more or less literally. If she was going to be unplugged, she'd do it all the way, and perform completely solo. After all, it wasn't exactly a new idea for her; it was something she'd done for several years at the bars in Long Beach, waiting to be discovered.

There was, however, one person she wanted onstage with her. The person who, more than any other, had influenced her music— Bruce Springsteen.

"I used to go home from school, plug my eight-track in, listen to Bruce Springsteen, and dream," was the way she introduced him to the audience. "One of the things I dreamed about was someday singing with him. So when this came up, I thought, 'What would happen if I asked?' So I did. And you know what? He said yes!"

Out of an amazing twelve months, this stood as the pinnacle for her, sharing a stage with the Boss, the two of them with acoustic guitars, dueting on "Thunder Road," the song he'd written and which she'd sung in concert so often.

"It was weird, frightening, and the best thing I've ever done," Melissa recalled excitedly later in an article in *Musician*. "I'll never forget rehearsing with him because he was kind of nervous, and we really didn't know which song to do. So I asked him to do 'Thunder Road' with me and he said, 'Sure.' "

It was a piece he hadn't performed live in a long time, which led, ironically, to her teaching him the song. They also had to find a key that suited them both. Melissa had learned it in the original E and in A, but Springsteen needed to play it in F.

"So I had to learn it in F," she said, "and in rehearsal I kept going to D minor when I should have gone to A minor . . . So doing that, and remembering where I was supposed to sing, and looking at him singing and being totally blown away by being with him, made it a hard time. But it was the best."

During the taping, she was so intent on staring at him that she forgot a line, which meant they had to start all over again. Nonetheless, she said, "Man, this one goes in the book. I don't know if it gets any better than this."

It was the cap on a triumphant evening. Recorded before an invited audience at the Brooklyn Academy of Music on February 15, 1995, Melissa performed a total of twelve songs, covering the span of her recorded career, from "Bring Me Some Water" and "Occasionally" all the way up to "Come to My Window" and "I'm The Only One" as well as a song not included on any of her own records—"All the Way to Heaven"—which would appear on her next album (but which, along with "Occasionally," was not included when the show was aired).

Even taken all the way down to basics, Melissa showed that she was a complete rock 'n' roller. She didn't need a band to sound raw and exciting, to capture the essence of her music; it was all there within her. Give her a stage and a guitar and it would come alive, passionate and urgent.

No video of the show was ever made commercially available, nor was there an audio release of the recordings. But that fitted into the way Melissa viewed her career. There'd never been a collection of her videos, and perhaps a little more surprisingly, there'd never been an official live album, although various tracks recorded live had been appended to the CD releases of some of her singles.

Following the glory of her "Unplugged" show, there was only one thing Melissa could really do—go back on the road, this time abroad. She'd been a major star in Australia for a few years. Some parts of Europe loved her—it wasn't unusual there for her to find bras and panties thrown at the stage, or, on occasion, to see naked women dancing in front of her.

"During one show I watched this woman take off her bra right in front of me. I kept shaking my head, screaming, 'Don't do that! Don't do that!' "

It didn't work. At one show in Holland it was becoming so out of hand that she had to tell fans, "Stop it. You're scaring me, and you're going to need those things later when you go dancing." But even her plea didn't help; Melissa's very sexual performance just brought that out in some people.

Offstage, though, Melissa had generally avoided appearing in sexy poses. She was a musician, a serious one. If some people made a pinup of her, well, there was little she could do about that. But it wasn't something she wanted to encourage. It was hard enough for women to be taken seriously in the music business as it was. Glamour shots, poses, each one detracted a little from all the work she'd put in over the years.

Which was why, when she appeared naked on a poster, it caused a mild sensation.

It was Julie's idea. She'd been contacted by PETA, who were producing a series of ads with couples, protesting cruelty to animals in the fur trade, with the copy to read, I'D RATHER GO NAKED THAN WEAR FUR.

Julie, a vegetarian, was concerned about animal rights. Melissa had been a vegetarian for a while, converted by k.d. lang, but she'd slipped back to eating chicken and fish, and she'd never stopped wearing leather—two things she wanted PETA to be quite aware of when Julie told her she wanted to be involved in the project.

Melissa was assured that it wasn't a problem. She and Julie both knew they'd be posing to give the illusion of being naked, and that seemed fine.

"Once we got into taking the pictures," Melissa recalled in *The Advocate,* "Julie said 'Gee, I thought we were going to have a sign in front of us or something.' She didn't realize that we were going to be totally nude. But a couple of glasses of wine, and we were OK with it."

Nudity itself wasn't a problem for her—she'd already used partial nudity on one of her album covers. Once the slight buzz from the wine hit kicked in, neither she nor Julie were much bothered by the situation. It wasn't exploitative; in fact, the picture used in the ad was quite tasteful, hardly the stuff of macho rock images. The session went smoothly, and that, Melissa thought, would be the end of it. There'd be some oohs and ahs when the ad appeared, but no one would really care. Unfortunately, she was wrong. The letters of protest began to pour in.

People in the fur trade complained at Melissa's stance, as anyone might have predicted, but a backlash that hit her with more impact came from AIDS researchers, who used live animals in their research. Melissa had been very active in the campaign to fight AIDS; now she found herself caught between two camps. Initially it had all seemed black and white to her, a protest against the wearing of fur, "but the issue isn't that clear; it bleeds into all sorts of things. . . . my father died of cancer, and I've lost too many friends to AIDS. So I do believe in animals losing their lives to eradicate cancer and AIDS from our lives; I believe in that."

After the uproar faded, she made a decision: She wouldn't do any more "visible work" for PETA. It had been, she admitted, a mistake. As for Julie, Melissa said, she "will do what she feels she needs to do, and I will support her in that."

By now the road had almost become home to Melissa. The tours, it seemed, were getting longer and longer. During the summer of 1995, crisscrossing America yet again, the venues were becoming larger. But that was because *Yes I Am* was continuing to sell. The three million and four million marks had come and gone, and it still wasn't stopping. People wanted to see her, to hear her. But somewhere it had to end. She couldn't, and wouldn't, live forever off one album. She had new songs, mostly written on the road, that she wanted to record. *Yes I Am* was almost two years old. Playing the songs so often, it had to be harder to inject them with full meaning and resonance. It was time to move on to something fresh. So on July 9, after a show at The Summit, in Houston, Texas, Melissa was finally able to head home to relax and decompress in the new house she'd barely seen.

It had been a wonderful, magical ride. *Yes I Am* had catapulted her to true star status. All the fears she'd had about whether America would accept a lesbian rock 'n' roller had proved to be completely unfounded. The country seemed to have embraced her. She'd become a media darling. After thirteen years Melissa had become an overnight sensation, doing more or less the same thing she'd done at the beginning. Could it last? There was no easy answer to that question, but as *Yes I Am* ended up with five million copies sold in America alone, it was hard to believe that it would ever end. She'd gone from being the outsider, the girl edging her way into the boys' club, to being a full member, accepted, lauded, even imitated. She'd even extended a helping hand to a couple of women following the same stony path she'd traveled—Joan Osborne and Paula Cole—by having them open on legs of her tours, exposing them to large audiences (which for Joan would help her achieve a hit album and single, and several Grammy nominations).

"There was a point right as *Yes I Am* was being released that I thought, 'You know what? I missed it," Melissa recalled. "I'm not trendy. I'm not a part of any scene. How am I ever going to reach a different level.' But *Yes I Am* totally proved me wrong, and I'm never going to think like that again. . . . It was so great that there's not some magic wand that some person has to wave over a record to make it great; I can just do what I love and feel and hopefully that's what people want to hear."

She had reached that new level. In America she could fill stadiums. In Australia her concerts sold out almost as soon as they were announced. Europe loved her. Melissa had become the first female rock superstar. For almost two years she'd been a remarkably visible presence, touring, being interviewed, playing Woodstock, opening for the Eagles and Sting, playing endless benefits, being involved in charity work (for which she was honored by VH1).

"As the opportunities came along, we took them, and I was everywhere at everything," she explained. ". . . in my own heart, I have feelings about causes that affect me. AIDS is one of them, because I've lost many friends to it; women's issues; of course, gay rights and all that stuff, because it affects me personally. So I'm going to offer my time and energy to [those]. It just sort of all melded together . . . with the work and the personal stuff, and it was very visible."

But where could she go from here?

$\mathcal{N}$INE

The answer, it seemed, was deeper inside herself. When *Your Little Secret* was released in the fall of 1995, so many of the songs resonated with Melissa's past that they were more or less rooted in a place and time—her childhood in Kansas. It wasn't so much autobiography as archaeology, digging to try and uncover the essence, the soul of the Midwest.

That type of move wasn't quite new. In 1982, as his fame grew rapidly, Springsteen had backed away to release the deliberately uncommercial *Nebraska,* a completely solo record, spare and dark, that tried to look into America's shaded heart.

Your Little Secret wasn't exactly Melissa's answer to that—it was neither dark nor uncommercial—but she did expose herself in ways she'd never done before, holding up the things that had made her and staring at them, trying to make sense of them all.

"Songs like 'Nowhere to Go,' 'Shriner's Park,' and 'I Could Have Been You' pull out parts of me that I have not examined before."

*   *   *

Once again, she coproduced with Hugh Padgham. After the success of *Yes I Am*, it would have been ridiculous not to have asked him back. The biggest change was that Melissa chose to use her touring band in the studio.

For a few years the musicians she'd used on the road had been different from the ones who'd back her on disc. Some artists chose to keep the two projects separate, to get a very specific sound in the studio using session musicians, then let things be much freer and looser in concert.

But after so much touring, Melissa's band had become a very tight unit, both musically and socially. With so many of the songs for *Your Little Secret* written on the road, and then arranged during soundchecks with the band, it just made sense to use them. They already knew the material. They were comfortable with it.

Her lead guitar player, John Shanks, a man who had a strong reputation as a writer himself, having composed hits for Joe Cocker, Bonnie Raitt, and others, cowrote a couple of tunes with her.

"It's the Mike Campbell–Tom Petty theory," he explained, referring to the partnership between Petty and his longtime guitar player. "And if it's something that excites her, she'll run off. She heard my track for 'I Could Have Been You' on the bus to Biloxi and said, 'That one's mine.' The next day she sang me the song, and I got chills."

A trust had built up between the two of them after playing together for so long. Melissa was willing to listen to John, and take his advice about guitar sounds. Much of the album was recorded live in the studio, the technique that had worked so successfully for her in the past, bringing a real presence and brightness to the music. For the title track it was his Les Paul guitar coming through the left speaker, and Melissa's Fender Telecaster on the right, both played through older tube amplifiers, giving a warm, complementary sound.

The one thing she'd chosen to put completely out of her mind was trying to write another "Come to My Window" or "I'm The

Only One." She herself would never have predicted either song would be a hit, so how could she write for the charts? All she could do was put down what was inside, "which is being on this journey and writing about it and doing it. . . . You just have to stay focused and not get caught up in it." She also had to put aside any feelings of pressure to release another bombshell of a record.

"I felt more pressure for *Yes I Am* where I really wanted to find something that would break through, something that would reach out, yet still be true to myself. It was a sign that I could write songs that I felt strongly about, that I could make the record with this band that I've been playing with, and enjoy it."

Although she'd come a long way, Melissa *still* wasn't ready to address a love song to a woman.

"True," she replied when asked about it, "but without being gender-specific in my songs, I think I'm becoming more sensual. Whereas before I might have shied away from using feminine descriptions, I feel freer in my writing—even though I'm not saying 'I love *her*.' "

But she did at least finally talk about being gay, albeit slightly obliquely, in "I Could Have Been You," which stood as a very personal plea for understanding.

"That is the basis for the song," she admitted to *The Advocate*. "It's about confronting someone who lives with that sort of intolerance. In a way, though, it could also be about racial intolerance. . . . you could stick religion in there or anything. I was just writing from *my* experience."

Writing so much from herself and her past, and putting the obsessive songs somewhat on the back burner was a challenge in itself. As a progression, it was artistically good; but it meant that the actual act of writing could sometimes be much harder.

"I almost gave up on 'Shriner's Park.' It just took forever to write. I was feeling that nobody's gonna want to hear about some old park that I used to go to when I was a kid."

The effort was worthwhile. On *Your Little Secret* Melissa produced some of her strongest lyrics, both bittersweet looks at her past and a promise for the future. By being willing to throw herself open in the songs, she'd liberated herself in many ways. Maybe it essentially mythologized a place and a time—the Kansas of her youth—but it also made them into American archetypes, much as Springsteen had done with the New Jersey of his adolescence. They both offered markers that everyone could identify with, the yearning to be an adult, to escape the restrictions of childhood, to be grown and to hit the road and be free. She'd touched on the edge of the subject before, in "You Can Sleep While I Drive" from *Brave and Crazy,* but here she plunged headlong into it.

Not that the obsessive songs that had become Melissa's trademark were completely absent from *Your Little Secret*—four of the ten cuts on the album dealt with problems in love. But she was widening her horizons, looking deeper within and discovering who she really was, exploring the depths she'd left untouched before, truly maturing as a writer.

Far more than her previous albums, *Your Little Secret* was a real band album. This time the only guest was John Mellencamp's drummer, Kenny Aronoff, who played on two tracks. Otherwise the players were her touring outfit: John Shanks on guitar and keyboards, Mark Browne on bass, and Dave Beyer on drums and percussion, while Melissa handled acoustic and electric guitars, as well as keyboards on the closing song "This War Is Over," making for a natural interplay and empathy between the musicians that came across on the record.

"I enjoyed making this record more than any other record I've ever made," Melissa said. "It came smoothly, it was fun, the guys I work with are a blast. I had a certain confidence. I think what you hear is that confidence. You hear me feeling, 'This is okay, I like playing this.'"

Most certainly, it wasn't a formula album, an attempt to duplicate *Yes I Am.* In its own way, it was every bit as experimental as *Never Enough,* but in a different way, exploring more personal lyrical avenues, and generally keeping the volume a little lower. Indeed, the only two out-and-out rockers were right at the beginning of the disc, the title track (which was also the first single), stripped-down and electric, with a big drum sound at the front of the mix, and "I Really Like You," which strongly recalled the frenetic pace of "Exile on Main Street"–era Stones, teetering on the very edge of chaos without tipping over.

The extremely autobiographical "Nowhere to Go," with its references to Leavenworth's prison and to cars (including the blue Chevy in which Melissa had left Kansas) brought to mind Springsteen's recent work, with sustained minor chords on the keyboard underpinning the whole song, drawing the listener into her words. Still, she'd always been influenced by Bruce; there was no reason that should end just because she'd become a star in her own right. The influence wasn't something that pervaded the whole disc.

"An Unusual Kiss" was more typically Melissa, building from a verse backed by acoustic guitar into a fiery, crunchy chorus of guitars and drums, building up a head of steam before letting John Shanks explode into a guitar solo. It was a style that had worked for her in the past, although for the first time, this record contained a number of real guitar solos, on seven out of ten songs—further evidence that she really trusted her players enough to let them have their say.

"I Want to Come Over," which would be the album's second single, opened with an introduction inspired by U2's early work before turning into a real pop song, one of the most obvious Melissa had ever written, once again heavy with keyboard washes under the sound, filling it out and swelling it. "All the Way to Heaven" appeared much as she'd sung it on the "Unplugged" show, completely acoustic, in a brisk march tempo, seductive in its simplicity, with the drums doing nothing more than keeping time behind the acoustic guitar, the overall effect wistful and harking back, rather than looking ahead.

"I Could Have Been You" was, perhaps, the strangest piece on the album, changing from soft, jazzy chords in the verse—not something Melissa had used before—to the pounding rock of the chorus, all the while keeping a slow, skillful beat that managed never to drag. It was the kind of tune she could only have pulled off with people who knew her well, whose connection to her went beyond the studio. On the surface it shouldn't have worked—the elements were too disparate—but it did, and even the whistling as the song ended didn't sound out of place. It needed to be heard a few times, though; on first listening, the music tended to distract from the lyric, one of Melissa's most personal, and certainly most topical, dealings with bias and intolerance.

"Shriner's Park," which had proved so difficult to write, was a wordy song, another turning of the page on Melissa's own adolescent experiences, an acoustic ballad whose tension grew slowly, with the band coming in for the second half of the song, but never overpowering the reflective, slightly somber mood. And "Change" was exactly that, upbeat, another pop song, with guitars playing arpeggios in the "jangly" style that REM had made so popular over the years, and, by Melissa's standards, another very commercial-sounding tune.

To close the record on a slower, more thoughtful pace, "This War Is Over" worked around a rhythmic figure, building the song from that, a ballad that brought to mind some of Peter Gabriel's more recent work with its full, plaintive sound and unforced emotionalism.

At this stage it was really a daring record to make. Many artists would have been perfectly content to reproduce a winning formula, and most of Melissa's fans probably wouldn't have complained if she'd done exactly that. Instead, she chose to progress, to make subtle changes, to bring in other flavors and textures to her music. It borrowed elements of what was beginning to be called "modern rock"—those touches of U2, Gabriel, and REM—and mixed them with the style Melissa had honed and refined. It stood as a continuation, a move along the path, familiar enough overall to be easily accepted by her audience, but using enough new sounds and touches to almost redefine her, and possibly bring in an entire new crowd to the music. *Yes I Am* had been the culmination of everything she'd achieved to that point, the real refinement of her style, the record of a musician whose time had finally come. *Your Little Secret* moved well beyond that, to the point where it was almost the start of a new era.

To be true to her artistic muse and the concerns that moved her, that was inevitable.

"Songwriters and artists are the mirrors of our society," she noted in *Musician,* "and it's our job to reflect it so we are constantly feeding on the collective consciousness of everybody."

She'd worked so hard for so long to become successful. Now that she'd achieved that, she'd made it clear that she wasn't about to stop moving and growing, either as a writer or performer.

Though having offered support, and helping her achieve success after those years of hard work, critics now seemed ready to indulge in the Melissa Etheridge backlash, as if her fame had suddenly made her a valid target. In *Entertainment Weekly,* Chris Willman stated his position at the start: "Excessive emotionalism's lone champion, Melissa Etheridge, continues to pound out the Women Who Love Too Much message with *Your Little Secret,*" and called her rock "musical comfort food for boomers . . ."

He was at least willing to acknowledge that she did "aspire to a more mature, singer-songwriterly style," but felt that her "middle-America minutiae could've been picked at random out of a CAT tractor hat," concluding that her "flame-broiled passion and want would seem to point in just one direction: the next meeting of Overstaters Anonymous."

Nor was *People* any kinder, finding her "still stuck with that unfortunate Janis Joplin complex . . ." and complaining about the "bombast," and "dramatic overkill."

It wasn't the most hopeful way to launch a new record, but Melissa may not have even seen the reviews. By the time they appeared she was already on the road, promoting the album in Australia, opening once again for the Eagles. In fact, for the first six months after the release of *Your Little Secret*, Melissa would barely have a chance to set foot in the United States, all part of a master plan to make her a major international star.

"Her career has focused on America," a representative at Island Records explained, "and we're not totally dismayed that, outside of a few territories, Europe and the rest of the world haven't embraced her the way people have here. We should afford her the opportunity instead of making her pound the album home here."

She was already huge in Australia, Canada, Germany, and Holland, but there was still so much of the world that hadn't received the message, especially Britain, whose music press was the most influential in the world. Much of January 1996 was to be spent there, playing shows and talking to journalists.

"We think Melissa's made the right record [for the U.K. market] for the first time," Island said. She had established an audience, but it remained small, in the region of twenty thousand people who'd buy every record, and "until we have her here and can get radio excited about her, it's terribly difficult to go beyond that fan base."

No American tour was booked until summer, 1996 (although Melissa would cross Canada in late winter). On the surface it seemed like an odd strategy, to ignore the country where her fans were the most ardent and go gallivanting off in search of global fame. But there was a certain logic behind it. Historically, the sales for her records began slowly, gradually building over the course of a year. *Yes I Am* had been the exception to the rule, but even that had continued to sell over a long period—after two and a half years it was still on the charts—rather than flaring briefly and dying, as so many artists' releases did. Her name would carry initial sales for six months, and when she began touring in the United States, they'd continue. The results out of the blocks were encouraging. Within three months, a million copies of *Your Little Secret* had been sold in America. Hardly the five million of *Yes I Am*, but with few live appearances to back up the record, it remained a good, strong figure. The video for the title track, the first single, saw plenty of airplay on VH1, and even MTV, a combination of live footage of Melissa and her band, combined with some very steamy scenes of a woman climbing a wall of bodies, and two women kissing—daring by television standards, and thus quite memorable.

Although Melissa wasn't touring America immediately, her presence wasn't entirely absent from its shores. She remained the darling of VH1, and inaugurated their new "Duets" series, aired just two weeks after *Your Little Secret* appeared in the stores. Filmed at Doheny Mansion in Los Angeles, on the campus of the College of Mount St. Mary's, it paired her with Joan Osborne, whom she'd come to know very well after they'd shared several months on the road; Sophie B. Hawkins, whose songs were every bit as sensual and even more explicit than Melissa's; and young singer-songwriter Jewel. Melissa wasn't familiar with Jewel's work, but coming with the recommendation of VH1 (the station Melissa had once jokingly called VMEH-1, for "video Melissa Etheridge hits"), she quickly accepted her.

The show also gave her a chance to play with the band, airing material off *Your Little Secret*. With "Duets" and "Unplugged," it was obvious that she'd now become a big enough star to draw television attention under her own name.

There was an irony in that; when all the Class of '88 women had appeared, it had been Melissa who'd received the least attention, who'd been perceived as the most mainstream, and therefore the weakest. But of all the names from that list—Toni Childs, Tracy Chapman, Edie Brickell, Michelle Shocked—Melissa was the only one who'd gone on to become a massive international star.

"I was just kicking and screaming and wondering why I wasn't selling a million records," Melissa recalled. " 'What's the matter with me? What's wrong with me?' . . . Looking back, I'm glad it happened like this. I'm so glad I'm coming into my own now. I'm a multimillion seller and I have this respect and this repertoire. And those who went boom are already over."

Melissa had finally blossomed into someone who had to be acknowledged. Even many of those who didn't care for her music respected her for having the strength to come out, to stand up and be counted. Over the course of 1994 and 1995 she'd broken through commercially, and come into her own as an artist, both big achievements. That did mean "a little loss of personal freedom," but it was, she realized, "a very small price to pay."

She readily admitted that coming out had been the big turning point. Not so much because her great success seemed to arrive after that, but because "I could really be 100 percent there for my success. I wasn't closeted and I didn't feel like there was stuff that wasn't being acknowledged. I didn't have to constantly worry and think, 'Well, but if they knew this other stuff about me, then it wouldn't have happened.' "

Perhaps the cap on it all was when *The Advocate* named her "Person of the Year" for 1995. Earlier in the decade the magazine had canceled an interview with her because she wouldn't talk about her sexuality, and now, in a short time she'd become important enough to warrant such an award. More than virtually any musician, she was a symbol of gay success in the business. While she continued to insist "I'm a musician who happens to be gay," the fact that she was a lesbian was one of those things people remembered about her and associated with her. There was no getting around it. It had put not just her career, but her whole life under the spotlight, and she'd handled it gracefully, never attempting to be anything other than who she was, a woman from a small Kansas town who'd worked hard, written some rock 'n' roll songs, and had some lucky breaks along the way. There was no star attitude. She remained the girl next door in her flannel and jeans (or sometimes the flashy leather pants of her stagewear); the only difference was that she was the girl next door who happened to be a lesbian and open about it.

Being chosen as Person of the Year was full acceptance by the community she'd long been a part of, and a recognition of what her success had done for the gay community. Even more than k.d. lang, Melissa had been the visible lesbian presence in music, the point person. She may have had little in common musically with very alternative bands like Tribe 8, an avowedly lesbian group, or even the gay Pansy Division, but without her to blaze the trail it remained debatable how much acceptance they might have had.

Certainly, since she'd come out there had been a growing number of out gay musicians and bands. The short-lived Riot Grrl movement had been very queer-friendly. Members of the Breeders and Hole had come out. At Lollapalooza '95 there had even been a "Dollars for Dykes" booth, set up to raise money for lesbian health causes and other issues. From the love that dare not speak its name, it had become, if not something to shout from the rooftops, then at least simply a part of life, not vilified as it had been in the past. In Hollywood being gay was even coming to be seen as commercially viable, with a big budget adaptation of *La Cage Aux Folles*, retitled *The Birdcage* and starring Robin Williams—a heterosexual actor—receiving a major release at the beginning of 1996, and going on to be the top-grossing movie in the country for several weeks.

Melissa could hardly claim credit for all of that, but she'd been one of the first to break down the barriers, to be welcomed into the established pantheon of stars. She'd helped, in her own small way, to make people see that gays weren't really different, that homosexual didn't have to mean drag queen or bull dyke.

While she chose to see herself primarily as a musician, her candor was perhaps as great a contribution as anything her songs had offered. The fact that she was an out, proud lesbian with a high public profile made her implicitly political. In contemporary America that was impossible to avoid.

Not that she'd fulfilled all her ambitions. There were still years of developing her music ahead of her, and, as with a number of musicians, acting remained intriguing to her. She had already had that very brief taste of it in 1985, but more recently there had been talk of her starring in a possible movie about the life of Janis Joplin. With an ongoing battle over who owned the rights to the Joplin story, though, it seemed unlikely that it would ever be made, at least with Melissa in the starring role—for, as she pointed out, "I think it better be resolved soon or else I'm gonna have to play a really old Joplin. She was only 27 [when she died]." With Melissa now thirty-five, she didn't have too much time left, but she'd taken on an agent to look into other film possibilities.

Her ambitions extended beyond work and career. There were two things that she and Julie truly wanted. One was to be married, not in the type of ceremony currently available for same-sex couples, but legally, with all the benefits available for that union. After seven years together, it still was not an option that was open to them, and it made Melissa understandably angry.

"Believe me," she told *The Advocate,* "the first state that legalizes same-sex marriages, I'm there, Julie's there, and we're getting married. We're first in line."

It wasn't simply for financial reasons, although there was no doubt it would help Melissa's "huge tax situation." Within society, it remained the ultimate expression of commitment, and that was what they wanted to show. They'd been together longer than many heterosexual marriages lasted, but they were still denied the chance to say "I do" under law.

Sometime in the near future, she and Julie also wanted to become parents. It was something they'd discussed for a long time, and were both set on it. Rather than adopt (as Julie's parents had done—until

Julie was twenty-four, she didn't know who her biological parents were), one of them—or possibly both—would get pregnant.

Although Melissa refused to say "how, who, when, or where," they were determined that it would happen. She did realize, though, that "having a child would mean I would have to be ready to take a lot of time off—which I can't do now. I'd have to wait until there wasn't such a demand on my time."

And the situation would inevitably return Melissa and Julie to the critical spotlight. As Melissa pointed out, "People who have been going, 'Fine, fine, they're gay, that's great,' are suddenly going to be going, 'Wait a minute—*they're* raising children?' "

However, she felt very strongly that gay people made good, sometimes even better parents, than straight couples.

"They think that we're horrible to children, that we shouldn't be teachers and parents, that there's some horror going on. I think that the more gay parents raise good, strong, compassionate people, the better the world will be."

The insemination, Julie said, would be "by a donor that we both knew."

If it happened, it would obviously involve huge changes in the way they lived, shifting the focus of their relationship as a baby inevitably will. Perhaps this was a cause for their hesitation, with Julie thinking it might be better to wait until "after I make two more movies," and she'd become fully established as a director. Simply because of the restraints imposed by biology, however, their decision has a time limit. All the details had been worked out; they have simply chosen not to make them public.

"I have let the world in on so much of my private life," Melissa said, "so this is the one area that's going to remain private. Although," she observed, "at some point people are going to know. . . . But we need to be in total control of it."

It wouldn't be impossible to combine music and parenthood—many others have successfully managed it—but it wouldn't be easy, either, especially given the amount of time Melissa has always spent on the road. That's hard enough on a relationship between two adults. With a young child added to the equation, the situation would inevitably alter. Something would have to give.

Could Melissa forget her career for a year or two? When all the touring for *Your Little Secret* is done could she sweep music aside for a while to concentrate on something else? It's difficult to imagine. After all, it's been so much a part of her daily life since she was eight years old. It's what she knows. It might mean that she'd become purely a recording artist for a while. But the fact still remains that she loves to play live. It's as big a thrill for her as it is for her audience. Giving all that up would chafe on her.

Now that she's firmly staked out her niche and become a real success, a bona fide star after years of work, of constantly proving herself, would she be willing to risk throwing it all away?

These are all questions she's certainly asked herself, things she's talked over with Julie, since the future hinges on them. The decisions they reach together remain to be seen.

Since coming out, Melissa—and, to a lesser extent, Julie—have been paired in the gossip columns with almost every out lesbian celebrity, all the way to Martina Navratilova. As Julie observed, "It's like whenever anyone comes out, they've automatically slept with Martina."

But the truth is that Melissa and Julie have always been a solidly monogamous couple. Each is the rock for the other, and that foundation has certainly helped Melissa's success. The groupies who gather around the tour bus—many male, as well as female, hoping she might change her mind, if only for a night—are ignored.

Melissa and Julie are not a wild party couple, seen everywhere, at everything. Home is where they tend to stay, living in a moderate style surrounded by their pets—cats, dogs, and birds. They see friends, who do mostly tend to be celebrities, but it's all in private, not parading for the paparazzi.

Ultimately, private sums up who Melissa really is. She's the Midwest girl who had the music in her, who kept the values of the place she was from. Always honest, pushing out the pain through her songs. What you see with her has always been what you've got. It never occurred to her to be otherwise. Coming out might have been a hard thing to do, but it was telling the truth, one of those great heartland virtues, and when it was told, as she said, "Well, you get what you give."

Honesty really could be the best policy.

*C*ONCLUSION

*I*n the years to come, how will Melissa Etheridge be remembered? For her own music, the heated intensity of her songs about sexual obsession? Or as a trailblazer for the cause of women in rock?

Whether it's for either or both, only time can tell. What is certain, though, is that she's earned her place in the musical history books. She's broken down barriers, and worked long and hard enough to gain her own position at the pinnacle of rock 'n' roll, up there with the artists she listened to when she was younger. And as a woman she's had to work twice as hard to do it, touring relentlessly, maybe not always being taken as seriously by the men, but always reacting in that polite, midwestern fashion, the way she was taught as a kid.

But as much as she's given to music, it's returned a great deal to her. It was, almost literally, her salvation. As a girl it was the only outlet she had for the tumble of emotions in her brain and her heart, all the things that were never spoken about at home. Writing and singing were therapy, particularly to a teenager who finally realized she was a lesbian, but who lived in a place and time where she couldn't be open about it.

Her gender-free lyrics were always her cloak. Even after she came out, she saw no need to throw it away. Her words had already caught people. Whether they knew it or not, by reacting they were admitting that lust, desire, heartbreak, betrayal, all the emotions connected with love, were the same for gay and straight people. Melissa's words were inclusive, rather than exclusive, utterly human. Her greatest contribution may have been to bring people of all sexual persuasions together with her songs, to do a little bit toward making them understand that whatever the label given to them, people were basically the same.

That's no small achievement in a world rife with divisiveness.

She's an artist whose growth can be easily plotted by her albums, from the eager rawness of *Melissa Etheridge,* which seemed like a last chance at the time, to the commercial riskiness of *Never Enough,* and then the massive breakthrough of *Yes I Am,* which brought together all the strands she'd explored in one triumphal package, to *Your Little Secret,* where she was willing to delve more deeply into herself and her own history, and to try and push forward musically, widening her range yet again.

"In your twenties you think you know everything," she explained. "And then you find that you don't, and there's a real freedom in that. Turning thirty wasn't traumatic for me—it was a marker for more to come. And it's just been better every year. . . . I'll tell you, I have lots of plans and lots to do, and I have an exciting life."

At thirty she was barely starting. Now, in her midthirties, Melissa has really caught her stride. For many in rock, by that time their careers are long gone, and they're either resting on whatever laurels they've garnered or they're back working in some obscure job. The artists with depth and resonance continue. They're the ones who are able to mature in what is generally an immature medium, who have something to contribute to music. She is one of them, a person still uncovering herself and the world, with something to say that matters, that people want to listen to.

While coming out gave her a great deal of visibility—and, whether she wanted the coverage or not, it *was* big news in the entertainment industry—she's gone to great lengths to point out that she's a musician who happens to be a lesbian, rather than a lesbian musician. While many girls and young women look up to her, even idolize her, as a lesbian figurehead, the idea of being any kind of role model is one she rejects.

"I have made mistakes," she said. "And I think I should be allowed to. If my life can be an example, great, but people should live their own life and live their own path."

Whether she wants it or not, though, many do see her as a focal point, as one of the most public lesbians in America. Even more than k.d. lang, who has tended to keep a lower profile, Melissa is in the spotlight. She receives the sackloads of fan mail, much of it from young women. She gets the bras thrown onstage (although she joked that her band would prefer diamonds, or possibly annuities). And when an article told of Julie's passion for collecting bowling balls, the packages of round, shiny objects began to arrive.

Within a certain segment of her audience, she inspires extreme devotion. But short of moving outside the musical mainstream, who else is there for these fans? Not only does Melissa remain the only out lesbian in rock 'n' roll, she is one of the very few women to have made an impact and sold several million records. *Yes I Am* continues to have an impact, even after the release of *Your Little Secret*. In May 1996, Melissa received the Songwriter of the Year Award from ASCAP (the American Society of Composers, Artists, and Performers) for the songs "Come to My Window," "I'm The Only One," and "If I Wanted To."

In the years to come it's almost inevitable that a new, major female performer will cite her as a big influence. She's shown that women can rock as hard, and with as much commitment, as men.

The Grammys sitting on the mantlepiece and the collection of platinum and gold records on the wall all testify to her growing acceptance, and to the fact that Melissa has made it in the business and broken through to join the ranks of the establishment. Those, and the thousands of people who come out to see her on the tours that grow larger and larger, are the obvious, outward signs of her success.

But real success, the personal sense of achievement, is within. And she's reached that, too. She's found a solid, lasting relationship that can be the foundation of her life. She's never stopped growing, both as a person and as a musician. After *Yes I Am* it would have been easy to have followed a similar formula for *Your Little Secret* and let the cash registers ring. Instead, she avoided that dead end and pushed herself—the mark of a real artist.

Still, more than any material trappings or adulation, it's her love of Julie that brings satisfaction. While Julie might be, in her own words, "a good example of the musical listening of the average Joe," she's been there for Melissa from the moment they got together, in 1990. Even when they were both working on projects, or during the long periods that Melissa has been on the road, there's never been any doubt between them. That's love, and it leaves them both very happy. The happiness is far more important than any career, because it can last a lifetime. So when Melissa said, "I'd do anything for her. If I had to choose, the career would be the thing I'd give up," it wasn't a token speech, but considered and real. For Melissa her relationship with Julie is her solid rock, the constant in her life that she can always rely on. Too many other things are ephemeral—even fame isn't guaranteed to last—but her relationship can. She knows she has to keep working at it, and that it's not easy. But she makes the effort, because she knows that in the long run it will all be worthwhile.

What does the future hold for Melissa? After a year promoting *Your Little Secret*, there'll be a rest, of course. From there, though, it's all wide open. The Janis Joplin film project looks unlikely, although Melissa confirmed that she has been talking to "people" about it. If it does happen, filming would take place in the summer of 1997. Acting remains a strong possibility, as she's stated.

"I've always wanted to do that," she acknowledged. "So I've been looking around a little bit. I don't want to play the part of, you know, 'the rock 'n' roll singer.' " Given that her first national exposure, in 1985, was acting, albeit in a tiny part on television, it's quite likely that she'll investigate the opportunities open to her. At this stage her name would have some marquee value, perhaps not enough to be the star, but for a featured role. And she has plenty of friends who are big names in the business, like Brad Pitt, Gwyneth Paltrow, Laura Dern, Jeff Goldblum, and Juliette Lewis (indeed, both Lewis and Paltrow, Brad's former and current flames, have taken roles in Melissa's videos)—people with clout, whose names help projects get made. Would Melissa come across on screen? Would she have real movie presence? She's spent years onstage, projecting. Her videos show that she films well. All that would need testing are her acting skills.

In Julie, she even has a director she can do more work with, just to keep things in the family, although Julie would likely prefer to move more toward commercial films, having had the experience of organizing everything, and working on a very tight budget for *Teresa's Tattoo*.

Acting is a feasible option for Melissa. But even if that did happen for her, it would never replace music as the creative outlet in her life. Even if she were a full-time parent, the music-making wouldn't disappear completely. It couldn't; it's just too important to her. As she continues to grow, and to evolve musically, the tale won't stop. In many ways she's just beginning to find herself musically. Her work grows more and more interesting and involved with every record. She's really only just started to move beyond the sexual and emotional obsessions that dominated her early records and plumb the depths of herself, her background, and the world around her. Like John Mellencamp and possibly Bob Seger, she has the ability to mine the consciousness of the heartland, to speak directly to it and from it, but with a unique perspective—that of a woman. While she may never make a record like Bruce's *Nebraska*, so stark and shadowy, or even like his *The Ghost of Tom Joad*, she has her own ways of getting at the truth, of inhabiting characters and hinting at their lives, their hopes, fears, dreams, and futures.

Whatever musical course she chooses to follow remains to be seen, but much of the material on *Your Little Secret* showed a writer becoming more serious about her craft and its effects, and capable of much greater things.

One short-term possibility, to keep her name alive in the media and the charts while she decides on her next step, would be a live record (although several live tracks have appeared on CD singles, and a few copies of *Yes I Am* came with a bonus live EP). Her shows have always been electrifying, intense, giving her and the band a chance to stretch out. The fact that many bootleg discs of her concerts exist indicates that there's no shortage of demand for them among her fans, and a live "best of" retrospective would satisfy a lot of people, especially if it was accompanied by a video.

In fact, nothing of hers has seen commercial release on video—neither the clips she's made for songs throughout her career, nor her "Unplugged" performance, which still gets strong viewing figures each time it's repeated on television. Melissa has never stated why she doesn't want them available, but many people would love to own them—especially the complete "Unplugged," with the two songs that never made it to the transmitted version.

It seems unlikely that they'll ever have the opportunity, beyond bootlegs. If any of these things were going to be made available, it would almost certainly have happened by now. This may end up being for the best, keeping the focus firmly on the new and the fresh, and letting the concerts be what they were always intended to be—ephemeral, magical moments people had to be there to really experience, be caught up in the excitement of the night, carrying the images in their memories rather than on video or disc.

Although she's had a hand in the production of all her records, even her debut, Melissa has shown no interest as yet in producing other artists, even the ones she's mentored to an extent, like Paula Cole (whom she wanted on the "Duets" show) or Joan Osborne. But production remains yet another avenue that's open to her, working with artists like those, or others with whom she might feel a connection.

Melissa Etheridge is nobody's little secret these days. It took the world at large a long time to really wake up to her talent. But having done so, it catapulted her into the superstar class, where playing in stadiums is not only something to aspire to, but the order of the day. Underneath all the L.A. trappings, though, the fast car and the big house, she remains the girl who grew up in the Midwest, polite to a fault, imbued with the values she applies to all her own dealings.

Five albums in eight years isn't a lot of material, just fifty songs. However, it's never been the amount that's mattered but how good they are, and the response they generate. Melissa's songs have always been about human connections, about an intense voice singing in a way no one has done in decades.

From being an outsider to the center of the charmed circle, she's come a long way. But her success has never been manufactured or bought. It was never based on fashion. She's worked her way to the top, touring endlessly, building up a solid fan base, until she finally achieved the critical mass necessary for her breakthrough. She's earned everything she's achieved. And that's what will keep her there. She doesn't take her success for granted.

Maybe she is the most visible, most popular lesbian in America, and, like it or not, coming out made her a symbol to others in the gay and lesbian community. Melissa and Julie will become even more visible following the official announcement of Julie's pregnancy, with a baby due in January 1997.

"It's a thrill of a lifetime," Melissa said in the press statement. "Both Julie and I have been planning this for a long time, and we couldn't be happier."

The performer who can give all of herself, in concert night after night, or on record, is a rare person. Melissa has gained that distinction. She cares, she's growing, maturing, and that's reflected in the songs she writes. She's become a rock 'n' roll *artist*. And that's why she'll be around for a long time.

AMERICAN DISCOGRAPHY

ALBUMS:

Melissa Etheridge (Island), 1988
Similar Features/Chrome Plated Heart/Like the Way I Do/Precious Pain/Don't You Need/The Late September Dogs/Occasionally/Watching You/Bring Me Some Water/I Want You

Brave and Crazy (Island), 1989
No Souvenirs/Brave and Crazy/You Used to Love to Dance/The Angels/You Can Sleep While I Drive/Testify/Let Me Go/My Back Door/Skin Deep/Royal Station 4/16

Never Enough (Island), 1992
Ain't It Heavy/2001/Dance Without Sleeping/Place Your Hand/Must Be Crazy for Me/Meet Me in the Back/The Boy Feels Strange/Keep It Precious/The Letting Go/It's for You

Yes I Am (Island), 1993

I'm The Only One/If I Wanted To/Come to My Window/Silent Legacy/I Will Never Be the Same/All American Girl/Yes I Am/ Resist/Ruins/Talking to My Angel

Your Little Secret (Island), 1995

Your Little Secret/I Really Like You/Nowhere to Go/An Unusual Kiss/I Want to Come Over/All the Way to Heaven/I Could Have Been You/Shriner's Park/Change/This War Is Over

*NOTE: A limited edition of *Your Little Secret* came with an extra live EP consisting of the tracks Come to My Window/No Souvenirs/ Ain't It Heavy/Yes I Am.

SINGLES:

Similar Features/Bring Me Some Water (Live)—Island, 1988

Like the Way I Do/Bring Me Some Water (Live)—Island, 1988

The Angels (alt. version)/The Angels (live)/Chrome Plated Heart (live)—Island, 1989

Let Me Go/Let Me Go (live)/Occasionally (live)—Island, 1989

2001/Meet Me in the Back (live)/Testify (live)—Island, 1992

2001/Meet Me in the Back (live)—vinyl, Island, 1992

Dance Without Sleeping/Similar Features (live)/Ain't It Heavy (live)—Island, 1992

Dance Without Sleeping/Ain't It Heavy (live)—vinyl, Island, 1992

I'm The Only One/Maggie May (live)/Ain't It Heavy (live)/I'm The Only One (live)—Island, 1994

Come to My Window/Ain't It Heavy (live)/The Letting Go (live)/I'm The Only One (live)—Island, 1993

If I Wanted To/Come to My Window (live)/Bring Me Some Water (live)/Like the Way I Do (live)—Island, 1995

Your Little Secret/All American Girl (live)/Bring Me Some Water (live)/Skin Deep (live)—Island, 1995

I Want to Come Over/Your Little Secret—Island, 1995

SOUNDTRACKS:

Weeds (Varèse Sarabande, 1987)—one track, "I Wanna Go Home."

Boys on the Side (Arista, 1995)—one track, "I Take You with Me"

COMPILATIONS:

For Our Children (Disney, 1991)—The Green Grass Grew All Around

Ain't Nuthin' but a She Thing (London, 1995)—Weakness in Me

Grammy's Greatest Moments Vol. IV (Atlantic, 1994)—Bring Me Some Water (live)

ONXRT: Live from the Archives Vol. 1 (WXRT, Chicago, 1993)—No Souvenirs (live)

A Little on the CD Side Vol. 11 (*Musician* magazine, 1993)—I'm the Only One

KZON Collectibles, Vol. 2 (KZON, Phoenix, AZ, 1994)—Come to My Window (live)

Classic Rock Box (WNEW-FM)—Like the Way I Do, On the Mountain, Vol. 1 (KMTT, Seattle, 1994)—Yes I Am (live)

Woodstock '94—I'm The Only One (live)

Women for Women—Dance Without Sleeping (Mercury, 1995)

It's Now or Never—The Elvis Tribute (Mercury, 1994)—Burning Love

MELISSA AS A GUEST WITH OTHER ARTISTS:

Don Henley—Melissa adds backing vocals to "Gimme What You Got" and "New York Minute" from *The End of Innocence* (Geffen, 1989)

Holly Near—Melissa plays guitar on "Singer in the Storm" from *Singer in the Storm* (Redwood Records, 1990)

Delbert McClinton—Melissa adds backing vocals to "Everytime I Roll the Dice" and "Can I Change My Mind" from *Never Been Rocked Enough* (Curb Records, 1992)

ACKNOWLEDGMENTS

No book is the work of a single person. All the way along the process others are involved. I'm very fortunate to have a wonderful agent in Madeleine Morel, who believes in me. Anne Savarese at St. Martin's Press went to bat for this project. I thank you. I owe so much to my parents, who first encouraged my writing, and to my wife and son, Linda and Graham, who make me think I'm at least getting something right in life. There are also the friends and family, Dennis Wilken, Mike Murtagh, all the Nagels and Watkins out there. And a massive debt of gratitude to Mary Hargrove, who took the time to search the Web and give me the results. Of course, no book of mine would be complete without a tip of the hat to Dave Thompson.

Thank you too to the wonderful people at *The Advocate*, for the long fax, and to *Out* for the same, even if, after repeated attempts, it never did come through. You were all more than generous.

The following articles proved very valuable in the writing of this book: "Melissa Etheridge," by Judy Weider, in *The Advocate*, January 23, 1996. "Melissa Etheridge: Rocking The Boat," by Barry

Walters, *The Advocate,* September 21, 1993 and (by the same author in the same publication), "A Rock Goddess Comes Out," April 20, 1993. "Melissa: Rock's Great Dyke Hope," by Judy Weider, *The Advocate,* July 26, 1994. "Melissa Etheridge: In Through the Out Door," by Rich Cohen, *Rolling Stone.* "Melissa Etheridge Takes the Long Hard Road from the Heartland to Hollywood," by Jancee Dunn, *Rolling Stone,* June 1, 1995. "Melissa Etheridge: Q & A," by Stacey D'Erasmo, *Rolling Stone,* June 2, 1994. "Melissa Etheridge's Little Secret," by Paul Zollo, *Musician,* January 1996. "The Pop Life," by Neil Strauss, *The New York Times,* December 14, 1994. "A Fiery First," by Michael Segell, *Cosmopolitan,* March, 1989. "A House in Harmony," by Peter Castro and John Griffiths, *People,* September 5, 1994. "Melissa Etheridge," by Ingrid Casares, *Interview,* October, 1994. "Rocker Melissa Etheridge, Who Is Both Acoustic and Electric," *People,* May 15, 1989. "Step Four: The Unplugged Melissa Etheridge," by Dana Kennedy, *Entertainment Weekly,* March 17, 1995. "Melissa Etheridge on Rock-Solid Ground," by Paul Verna, *Billboard,* April 4, 1992. "Etheridge Sells Out Major Market Engagements in U.S. and Canada," by Louise Zepp, *Amusement Business,* October 28, 1993. "Island Targeting Etheridge Abroad," by Melinda Newman, *Billboard,* October 18, 1995. "Island Ready to Build on Etheridge's '94 Breakthrough," by Larry Flick, *Billboard,* January 7, 1995. "Island's Melissa Etheridge Cracks Top 40 with Hit Set," by Brett Atwood, *Billboard,* December 10, 1994.

The Melissa Etheridge Information Network can be reached at PO Box 884563, San Francisco, CA 94188, or by phone at (415)597-6760. For those with computer access, two Melissa Etheridge Web sites exist: http://fantasylum.com/melissa/ and http://www.polygram.com/metheridge.